CRITICAL DESIGN IN CONTEXT

CRITICAL DESIGN IN CONTEXT

History, Theory, and Practices

MATT MALPASS

Bloomsbury Academic
An imprint of Bloomsbury Publishing Plc

B L O O M S B U R Y
LONDON · OXFORD · NEW YORK · NEW DELHI · SYDNEY

Bloomsbury Academic

An imprint of Bloomsbury Publishing Plc

50 Bedford Square	1385 Broadway
London	New York
WC1B 3DP	NY 10018
UK	USA

www.bloomsbury.com

BLOOMSBURY and the Diana logo are trademarks of Bloomsbury Publishing Plc

First published 2017

British Library Cataloguing-in-Publication Data
A catalogue record for this book is available from the British Library.

ISBN:	HB:	978-1-4725-7518-0
	PB:	978-1-4725-7517-3
	ePDF:	978-1-4725-7520-3
	ePub:	978-1-4725-7519-7

Library of Congress Cataloging-in-Publication Data
Names: Malpass, Matthew, author.
Title: Critical design in context : history, theory, and practices / Matt Malpass.
Description: New York : Bloomsbury Academic, 2017. | Includes bibliographical references.
Identifiers: LCCN 2016029739| ISBN 9781472575173 (paperback) |
ISBN 9781472575180 (hardback)
Subjects: LCSH: Design–Philosophy. | Design–Social aspects. | BISAC: DESIGN / General. | DESIGN / History & Criticism. | DESIGN / Product. | DESIGN / Industrial.
Classification: LCC NK1505 .M32 2017 | DDC 745.4–dc23
LC record available at https://lccn.loc.gov/2016029739

Cover image: Uncomfortable Chair 4, 2014
Image courtesy of Win Tianli

Typeset by Integra Software Services Pvt. Ltd.
Printed and bound in India

CONTENTS

LIST OF FIGURES

ACKNOWLEDGEMENTS

There are many people to thank for their support while writing this book and I am grateful for the contribution that many have made towards developing the account of critical design practice presented in the following chapters. To others, I am grateful for the support and advice offered during the process of research and writing. There are a few people that I must thank by name: First, Tracy Cordingley and Jamie Billing for introducing me to the field and setting me off on a form of inquiry with a direction and energy that sustain my interest in critical design practice today; Steve Rutherford, Hugh Miller, Tom Fisher, and Guy Julier for their insight and critical input in the formative stages of this project; and Lorraine Gamman, Adam Thorpe, Janet McDonnell, Nick Rhodes, Rebecca Ross, and the Design Against Crime team at Central Saint Martins for their support, for all the opportunities, and for affording the necessary culture in which to develop this work. I am grateful to Nottingham Trent University, and the University of the Arts London but especially to the staff and students of MA Industrial Design at Central Saint Martins who provided a day-to-day context for experimentation, a forum for debate, and a space to continually test ideas and thinking. For generously sharing their perspectives on the field over the past few years, my sincerest thanks go to Ralph Ball, Maxine Naylor, Anthony Dunne, Fiona Raby, Noam Toran, James Auger, Tobie Kerridge, Ramia Mazé, Kieren Jones, Nelly Ben Hayoun, Stephen Heyward, Bruce and Stephanie Tharp, and Jana Scholtz. My gratitude goes to all the designers who have generously contributed images of their work to exemplify the practice and illustrate the discussion. Thanks to Rebecca Barden for commissioning the work and the editorial team at Bloomsbury for their support throughout, to Heather Griffith for her input on early drafts, and to the reviewers for their critique and input in developing the manuscript. Finally, I would like to express my deepest gratitude to my family, Dianne, Paul, and Jonathon Malpass, Debbie and Andrew Moss, and Rita Lee for their enduring support and to Chloe Griffith for her support, critical acumen, advice, patience, and enthusiasm throughout. Thank you!

1
INTRODUCING CRITICAL DESIGN

Industrial design is typically perceived as the process of design applied to the development and manufacture of products for mass production and consumption. It is synonymous with companies, such as Apple, for their technological innovations wrapped in aluminium and glass casings, which millions consume, and millions more aspire to own and use. It is synonymous with furniture design conceived by the likes of Charles and Ray Eames, Arne Jacobsen, and George Nelson, designs that are now produced and distributed by companies such as Vitra and Herman Miller and adorn 'stylish' living rooms and offices in many cities around the world. It is synonymous with the innovative production and material processes developed by Kartell in their plastic products, Dyson in their vacuum cleaners, Artemide in their lighting, and Unilever in their packaging. It is synonymous with the stripped back modernist aesthetic of Dieter Rams for Braun, or Naoto Fukasawa for Muji. It is synonymous with such superstar designers as Marc Newson with a flash of orange as motif in his product design, Ross Lovegrove with his biomorphic obsessions, Philippe Starck with his love of compound curves, and Karim Rashid's pink blobjects. These examples of industrial design are conceived within a market-led paradigm. In this paradigm, the products of design are ultimately commercially orientated, designed, and produced for sale and use.

While industrial design practice might exist to drive production and consumption in a commercial paradigm, this is not its only application. Alternative models of industrial design exist to these mainstream practices. These models of practice are critical of orthodox applications within design practice; they are conceptual in their focus and challenging in their effect. This book is about such critical design practice.

In critical design practice, designers reject a role for industrial design that is limited to the production of objects conceived solely for fiscal gain and technological development. It seeks to avoid conventional production and consumption, offering an alternative use of industrial design. Instead, they propose that product and industrial design[1] can be used to mobilize debate and inquire into matters of concern through the creative processes involved when designing objects. They propose that the forms of interaction that occur within the design process, and through a user's engagement with design work, can bring into relief issues by the materialization of these issues in objects and the experiences afforded. Guided by this rationale, critical design practice aims to challenge the current state of industrial design. In critical design practice, the principles, methods, and tactics of design are extended towards an application for design that offers more than a service-based relationship between a client and a designer. In doing this, it applies strategies that challenge the limits of design. These designs act as a form of critique and argument that is established through the design of objects and through the communication of an object's narrative of use. This is achieved through processes of making and production, scenario building, and storytelling.

An increasing number of designers aim to present and define this approach. The practice has grown in popularity within the industrial design discipline over the past decade – particularly in an academic context of design research and postgraduate education. However, while there is much attention focused on critical design in practice, and where many examples of work populate exhibitions and design blogs, this book is amongst the first to theorize the field of critical design practice by presenting an overview. It considers the relationships between types of critical design practice, examples of design work, and the methods and tactics employed in practice. This is not to say it is the first book on critical design; there are a number of influential works written by practitioners who have worked to popularize and advance the field. There are increasing examples of researchers, design theorists, and critics working to understand and challenge the practice through academic articles, design writing, exhibition text, and the blogosphere. Notable exhibitions focusing on the practice include *Strangely Familiar: Design and Everyday Life* held at the Walker Arts Center, Minneapolis, USA, in 2003. This presented numerous examples of critical practice that blur the boundaries between form and function, questioned the habitual, and challenge hegemony within quotidian conditions. *AC DC – Art Contemporain Design Contemporain –* held in Geneva in 2007 brought designers, curators, critics, and academics together to question the influence of arts practice on emerging critical and conceptual forms of design. *Designing Critical Design* held at Z33, Hasselt, Belgium, in 2007 was the first exhibition to title an exposition of work as critical design. It brought together some of the main protagonists in the field including Dunne and Raby, Jurgen Bey, and Martí Guixé – examples of their work will be explored in later chapters. The following year in 2008 similar themes and examples were showcased at Somerset House in London in *Wouldn't It Be Nice … Wishful Thinking in Art and Design.* This provided a platform for Ryan Gander, Bless, Dexter Sinister,

Alicia Framis, Martino Gamper, Tobias Rehberger, Superflux, and Chosil Kil and brought these designers into the discourse surrounding the practice. The same year the exhibition *Design and the Elastic Mind* at the Museum of Modern Art, New York, curated by Paola Antonelli, provided perhaps the broadest and most inclusive showcase of examples. The exhibition included work familiar to the emerging canon, but went to include challenging and provocative examples of work from research labs, innovation centres, and student work. In working to popularize critical design and its relationship to mainstream design practices and contemporary art, these events were all celebratory in tone. Through the popularization of the practice, the gallery also became the place in which to design for and disseminate design work through.

Recently, a more focused critical discourse has emerged in the presentation and exhibition of work. For example, over summer 2014 as part of MoMA's *Design and Violence*, a project that invited curators to propose examples of work for an open online debate, the design writer John Thackara introduced *The Republic of Salivation* (2010) by Michael Burton and Michiko Nitta. The project depicts a dystopian future scenario and the consequences of global food shortage. A discussion emerged in response that challenged the insular discourse on critical and speculative design. It challenged the grounding of many examples of critical design asking if the propositions pay enough attention to the causes of threats that the work addresses or the hegemonies that they challenge. This line of thought argues that critical design practice often appears radical, but simply maybe masquerading as radical because of the violence and shock in the proposition that the designers make and the expectations of use that they fabricate. The debate echoed design scholars who have targeted critique at critical design's lack of engagement with discourse beyond art and design and how in within the practice designers are for the most part talking to themselves and peers and often fail to engage the root of problems and rather elaborately project fictional consequence. Tonkinwise's (2015) *Design Philosophy Papers* review of Dunne and Raby's (2014) *Speculative Everything: Design Fiction and Social Dreaming* presents and discusses the designers' work and methods, which appears at first to be acutely critical of critical design practice, its designers, and value of this design practice. Arguably, however, such a critique is delivered from a position of confidence in the value of critical and speculative design practice since it offers a call for the practice to stand up to the scrutiny in the critique laid out. In such events, we are starting to see serious and challenging questions being asked of the practice but equally the designers are responding to such critique and in such the practice advances and matures. This is healthy, since ultimately for critical design practice to be truly critical and offer value in extending the agency of design, to challenge disciplinary thinking, and to possibly even effect change, it must not be above critique itself.

Challenging orthodoxy

Critical design practice is one among a growing number of approaches that aim to present and define interrogative, discursive, and experimental approaches in design practice and research. Such approaches include research through design (Frayling 1993; Zimmerman, Stolterman, and Forlizzi 2010). This approach is commonly associated with design research and often carried out in academic contexts, presenting a critical epistemological pursuit through design practice. Strategies of ludic design (Gaver et al. 2004), reflective design (Sengers 2005), slow design (Hällnas and Redström 2001), and counter-functional design (Moline 2008; Pierce and Paulos 2014) each aim to slow the interaction with objects and afford meaningful and questioning engagement with the objects and services proposed by challenging ubiquitous interaction with product and services. Adversarial design (DiSalvo 2012) explores activist and politically engaged opportunities afforded when publics are brought together around an issue that is brought to attention through the introduction of boundary objects.[2] These design interventions are interpreted and made sense of through the active critical participation of users and stakeholder groups. Each of these approaches in their own right challenges governing mentalities and orthodoxy within design practice. The purposive function of the work has a social and political orientation, rather than a commercial focus, by empowering publics, questioning technology, and challenging expectation of use. In this respect, critical design practice shares its critical agenda but is less easily defined as a form of practice because of its popular understanding.

Challenging colloquialism:
The problem with critical design

Before entering the discussion into history, theory, and practice, it is important to address the colloquial and popular understanding of critical design. The colloquial understanding within design culture goes something like this: The term 'critical design' was coined by Anthony Dunne (1997), and it describes a form of practice that he and Fiona Raby developed as research fellows with colleagues at the Royal College of Art (RCA), London, in the early 1990s. Critical design is located outside terms set by capital or production and counters conventions of utility, technology, and fiscal gain. Produced for exhibit rather than sale, these designs are less about problem solving and more about problem finding within disciplinary and societal discourse.

A popular view exists that considers what Dunne introduces as critical design in *Hertzian Tales* (1997) – a key text in design literature – as being representative of the field. The term 'critical design' has since been adopted as an umbrella term for any type of practice that suggests product design offers possibilities beyond the solving of design problems. However, Dunne and Raby themselves express caution when using 'critical design' as a label:

> For us critical design now is a useful term to describe a practice that uses design as critique. But at the same time, we're very wary of it becoming a label or a kind of a shorthand. I think the idea of design as a form of critique is really important and special. I'm worried that the label critical design is too narrow a form. Obviously, that particular phrase came from us and characterises the type of way that we work. It would be much more exciting to see other forms of design that critique. That maybe challenges what we do or offer something different. (Dunne and Raby Interviewed by Author, 2009)

Dunne and Raby's 'critical design' has reconstituted the history of critical practice in product and industrial design. Other forms of conceptual design practice and other designers operating critically have ultimately come to be described as practising 'critical design'. This generalization has led to critical design having values applied to it that do not correspond with the intentions of some designers engaging in critical practice, as Pullin writes:

> I am never sure whether to use the term critical design to define my own work these days. The term is so associated with the Design Interactions course at the Royal College of Art, and its subversive, often dystopian, visions of technological futures. (2010, 324)

> I see as many parallels with the work of Bill Gaver's Interaction Research Studio at Goldsmiths – another group whose work is associated with critical design by observers, but not thought of as such by its practitioners. We haven't managed to come up with as compelling an alternative definition yet though. (Pullin 2010, 324)

While addressing the emergence and development of critical design practice as a distinct form of product and industrial design, this book aims to take a broad view of critical design practice within this context. It discusses critical design's emergence from a historic perspective. It explores the theoretical underpinning of the practice and the methods that critical designers employ within their work. It looks in detail at the mechanisms designers use to establish the critical move through design and engage audiences and users of their work in debate. Here, there is a particular focus on how designers marry product design practices with satiric narratives to create dark, humorous, and often ambiguous objects that encourage users to engage with themes critiqued by the designers.

The examples discussed will show how critical design practice is positioned as a form of socially and politically engaged activity and creative activism. The act of industrial design is used to incite reflection on issues pertinent to society today and designing is used as a medium for critique. Critical design practice challenges hegemonies and dominant ideologies in contexts of science and technology, social inequality, and unchallenged disciplinary norms.

The field is increasing in examples and exposure; however, as the number of examples increase, the theoretical analysis has until recently remained rather thin. For the practice to develop, more work is required that problematizes critical design and its methods. Throughout the book, the argument is made for the need to engage a broader readership in the discussion on critical design in order to engage a community of interest beyond the critical design practitioners that stoically advocate the practice. There is a need to develop the discourse on critical design practice beyond self-referential accounts, glossy design magazines, exhibitions, and coffee table publications that currently present and disseminate this field of practice. Therefore, *Critical Design in Context* offers an analysis of the practice and the contribution that critical design makes to the industrial design discipline and beyond. A specific strategy used is to broaden the range of examples and case studies in the book to delineate the antecedents of popular examples of critical design and to draw together literature within the discourse of critical design practice. Critical design is often placed as a UK-centric movement; while the UK, and London in particular, does produce a lot of this design activity, the book will emphasize the international diversity of practitioners engaging in the practice. The book includes a range of examples from across Europe and Scandinavia as well as the USA and Southeast Asia.

Because of the non-commercial and professionally challenging agenda of critical design, there are barriers to the uptake of the practice by the broader industrial design profession. The book aims to challenge these barriers and locate critical design practice in a disciplinary and professional context.

The book goes further to address a lack of understanding about the function of critical design and a growing impatience of the practice. It argues that in a time of austerity, where globally we are faced with rising complex societal problems, ethical sociotechnical questions, and material scarcity, there is need for a broader and more questioning form of design practice that serves to question industrial design practice, challenging governing mentalities within orthodox industrial design and striving to advance the role and agency of the industrial designer. It discusses how this non-commercial practice is supported and facilitated within design culture and through institutional relationships in academic and educational contexts.

What's so critical about critical design practice

Even though design and interaction with objects has a massive effect on our everyday life, a somewhat limited discourse has focused specifically on the effects of design from within the design profession, a claim supported by Miller's dismay of product design:

> It ought to be unimaginable that a profession would spend its entire time concerned with designing the particular form of goods without seeing it as essential to attempt to show what the consequences of that particular design would be. (2001, 1)

Critical design practice offers a means to use product design as a medium to focus on concerns both central to the discipline and beyond normal disciplinary bounds. The critical move is established by the voluntary insubordination of design methods. However, just as critical design practitioners challenge disciplinary orthodoxy and boundaries, in their insubordination they aim to develop a critical tradition that contributes to product design's disciplinary foundation, addressing Thackara's concerns that:

> Because product design is thoroughly integrated into capitalist production, it is bereft of an independent critical tradition on which to base an alternative. (1988, 22)

Within the field, a number of practitioners and academics have recognized problems with uncritical design practice and have mobilized product design as a specifically critical act challenging how mainstream design unthinkingly propagates the values, assumptions, and ideologies inherent in the designer who passively embodies these values in products. This practice is motivated by an impulse to reframe the circumstances surrounding contemporary product design by using modes of investigation that probe the boundaries of the discipline and challenge the prevailing perception of what product design is, how it operates, and what the designer is capable of using product design for.

Unfortunately, formal analysis of this reframing has not kept pace. Often critical design activity is not considered product design. Raby (2008, 96) writes that in the majority of instances it is described as art. This claim is further supported in my own experience, observations, and research into the field. For example, when attending design research colloquiums and symposiums that focus on critical design practice, the discussion with the audience will inevitably result in the question being asked 'isn't it just art?'. A function of this book begins to address this analysis. The intention here is to advance the debate in critical design practice beyond the question 'isn't it just art?'. In attempting to do this, a range of concepts, perspectives, and methods that facilitate the operation of critical design practice are exposed and discussed.

Why study critical design?

Throughout the book 'mainstream', 'traditional', 'orthodox', 'conventional', and 'affirmative' design are used to describe design activity that represents a governing mentality in product and industrial design. This mentality constitutes widely shared values, norms, and expectations of how product design operates. In mainstream design, the market provides strong incentives for designers to participate in economic systems that are arguably beyond individual's ability to confront.

There are numerous forms of design practice set outside what might be considered mainstream design. These include participatory design, co-design, design activism, feminist design, and, more recently, socially responsive and transition design. Consideration of these practices is important because it brings into light the interconnected constraints to agency for designers who seek to challenge the status quo and mainstream applications of product design. However, in contrast to the research that focuses on these practices, formal analysis of critical design practice has not kept pace. This is concerning as Dunne and Raby argue that:

> The design profession needs to mature and find ways of operating outside the tight constraints of servicing industry. At its worst product design simply reinforces global capitalist values. Design needs to see this for what it is, just one possibility and to develop alternative roles for itself. It needs to establish an intellectual stance of its own, or the design profession is destined to lose all intellectual credibility and viewed simply as an agent of capitalism. (Dunne and Raby 2001, 59)

Although Dunne and Raby's prescription for design was presented in the late 1990s, it continues to have resonance. Indeed, with the aid of hindsight, now more than ever critical practices in design need to establish an intellectual stance of their own or else they are destined to lose their intellectual credibility. More and more the danger is that critical practice becomes overly self-reflexive and introverted, sustained, practiced, and exchanged in a closed community. By operating in this way, its usefulness as part of a larger disciplinary project is undermined. Mazé identifies the problem with critical design practice if it is not taken up as a disciplinary project and highlights the danger that if there is no extension beyond commentary or critique, critical design 'might tend towards an overly self-reflexive and hermetic autonomy' (Mazé and Redström 2007, 8). So there are already utterances of critical practice being little more than 'design for design's sake', 'design for designers', or perhaps more appropriately 'design for critical designers'.[3]

In design research, where ideological bases rule and theoretical grounding are essential as reference points, critical practice has not been viewed as a serious form of design. It is sustained in a somewhat closed discourse limited to design magazines, niche publications, and gallery showcases. Its theorization and documentation is left to design journalists, bloggers, and curators whose primary agendas are arguably to sell magazines, accumulate hits, or to get the viewing public through gallery doors. Thus, there is a need for the constructive input of a broader community to develop the practice alongside critical designers as the vital form of product design in both disciplinary and professional contexts. Increasingly, this development must come about thorough critique and problematization of the practice itself. At the time of writing, the design studies' focus on critical practice is limited compared to that which focuses on other fields of ideation and making. This is evident in the lack of exogenous research that specifically addresses critical practice, notable when compared to the amount of scholarly writing that focuses on other marginalized practices.

Fields such as participatory design, socially responsible design, and co-design have emerged in parallel to critical design practice. These modes reflect upon the relationship between design and the communities that are being designed for, and, or with. They operate beyond conditions set by fiscal gain or technological development. They are established as intellectual and politically motivated practices, informing policy and used to address complex societal concerns. In their deviation from focusing on the production of objects, they reflect instead a move towards the designer acting as the facilitator for large groups of people; they imply a critique of mainstream design, or at least challenge common perceptions of the designer's role. They are assumed progressive within disciplinary discourse. They have been absorbed into the disciplinary orthodoxy through the shared efforts of theorists, commentators, and practitioners.[4]

Over the past several years, critical design practice has received increasing attention in design research, education, and practice but only recently in design research has critical design been viewed as a form of design where ideological basis and theoretical grounding are a requirement. Within design research, critical design practice ignited discussions of design as a method of cultural provocation where some designers and commentators take critical design as a starting point for discussing how social issues and political themes might enter design practice. But there have also been calls for a post-critical design that addresses limits of critical design, including its potential to reinforce rather than question and confront the status quo and how it applies piecemeal critical theory and is framed flippantly as being politically engaged. Essentially, these calls challenge how critical design is sustained and why it is of value. There is a continuing need for the constructive input of a broad community to question the practice as a useful form of product design in disciplinary and professional contexts. By presenting an overview of the field, this book begins to address this need. It is not overtly critical of critical design practice; it advocates the importance of critical design practice throughout. It aims to offer an introduction to the practice in order to broaden the readership and understanding of the practice. The book works to unpack the methodological approaches applied in practice and to provide analytical tools that can be used to question critical design practice.

Researching critical design practice

Product and industrial design now occupies a position where it is confident enough as a discipline to be a vehicle for fulfilling social needs and for expressing independent thought. Through a more design-focused criticism of critical design practice, the value of critical design practice and its contribution to the product design discipline might be revealed. Moline (2008) and Mazé (2007) state that without formal analysis and serious intervention from the design research community, critical design practice might be consumed as a purely superficial form of product design. They recognize the need for design to reflect on its own products and practice, and the impact of its products and practices as tools of inquiry and commentary, and address Bonsiepe concerns:

> We can hardly get to the root of design using art theoretical concepts. Design is an independent category. Located at the interface of industry, the market, technology and culture (living practice), design is eminently suited for engaging in culturally critical exercises that focus on the symbolic function of products. (Bonsiepe 2007, 30–31)

Activity focused in this way would address Raby's claims that there is a need for analysis of the practice to avoid it been seen as a form of design entertainment.

'Critical' in critical design practice

What distinguishes critical design from other forms of design is its criticality. But what model of criticality? There is a relationship between critical design practice and critical theory; however, in critical design practice, critical theory is arguably applied strategically and sporadically, using concepts for inspiration and explanation rather than attempting to construct a complete and internally consistent argument. Reference to a range of post-structuralist thinkers or philosophers in Science and Technology Studies places a considerable burden on the audience to infer how all of this theory adds up to ground a critical design practice. As a design practice, critical design is perhaps better understood in relation to recent design approaches that expand design methods, tactics, and strategies beyond generating consumer products. It is informed by a long history of creative practice, including Dada and Situationism. Such approaches first developed in Art where artists integrated playful forms of critique through the appropriation of everyday objects and the celebration and subversion of quotidian conditions. Informed by these traditions, critical design practice has drawn on tactics associated with art to orient a subversion of design norms. Informed by conceptual art, critical design practice might be described as shifting focus from designer and the object to the concept. The design process has moved to set up the design concept (through material thing, or improvised intervention, instillations, performance, user participation, or other means) to challenge idea, institutions, and audience. As conceptual art mounted a critique of art by challenging institutional frames, for example, transgressing the gallery through readymades and intervention art, critical design practice subverts the ingrained expectations of design, use, and technological progression. Critical designers draw on artistic methods to critique design, science, and social concerns. In many examples, they take over spaces traditionally reserved for art, placing design in the gallery to draw attention to these concerns. In this respect, critical design practice relates to the conceptual domain of art. Fundamentally, however, objects of critical design practice relate everyday rituals and conventions of use. Chapter 4 will explore how attempts to make distinctions between art and critical design are misguided. Critical design and art may or may not overlap, but that critical design, tactically speaking, should not be absorbed into the social practices of the artworld, with their institutional structures of exhibitions, museums, and funding. Rather, critical design works best when it is operating within a context of use.

Critical design practice also bares a relationship to activist approaches to design and making that question and reframe the social role of institutional practices of design e.g. socially responsive design (Thorpe and Gamman 2011), critical making (Ratto and Boler 2014), and transition design (Tonkinwise et al. 2015). So there is a 'critical' tradition in design and the arts that is largely independent of critical theory and philosophies of difference. If we frame being critical as necessary and exclusively understood through these textual traditions, we make it more difficult to understand where critical design practice is coming from. It is therefore important to question what criticality can and should do in design practice beyond the forms and traditions of criticism from the humanities and cultural studies. In attempting to do this, a range of tactics are explored throughout the book that inform the critical design practice either explicitly or intuitively in practice. Focusing on the form and operation of critical practice, the book provides a framework by which to analyse, differentiate, organize, and discuss the characteristics of work. Above all, it allows us to study the field's nuances and work towards a taxonomy of critical practice in design. It does this by providing contextual tools and theoretical apparatus that act as a point of access into the discussion of critical practice and its reflection in a variety of design projects. In doing this, I hope to argue for the value and necessity of this field of product and industrial design.

Industrial design as a discipline

It is important to acknowledge the transdisciplinary character of many of the approaches that will be discussed in the following chapters. Transdisciplinarity is an unavoidable characteristic of a practice that looks to engage other fields and expertise, and extend a disciplinary purview. Human Computer Interaction, Interaction Design, Graphic and Communication Design, and Media-Art are among the practices that have informed critical designs development in an industrial design context. Each of these fields has its own account of critical practice. However, to be transdisciplinary, interdisciplinary, or cross-disciplinary, one must be disciplinary first and formed in a discipline to then cross over into other disciplines. My position in relation to critical design and the approach taken in writing this book is informed by my experience as an industrial designer, first operating in a commercial context before moving to research and practice in a critical design context. Throughout the book, critical design practice is positioned and discussed as a field of practice within the discipline of product and industrial design. It focuses on critical design practice specifically as it is understood as a form of product and industrial design and how it emerged from practices of industrial design.

As a designer, academic, and educator, I consider product and industrial design as a discipline before I consider it a profession. Like Cross (2006) and Nelson and Stolterman (2012), I frame industrial design as a specific branch of knowledge, learning, and practice, and a discipline that incorporates expertise, people, projects, communities, challenges, studies, inquiry, and research areas that are strongly associated with industrial design. Disciplines develop through dialogue, inquiry, claims, and rebuttal. For a discipline to emerge, it requires challenge and a critique of hegemony, multiple interpretations, voices, and perspectives. It needs protagonists on the edge looking outward and protagonists within reflecting on the value of the core disciplinary practice. It needs its advocates and adversaries. I pose that critical design practice affords this to product and industrial design. Through this book, we will see how critical design operates, explore its tradition and lineage, and argue why it is important in a product and industrial design context.

Critical Design in Context serves to offer an introduction into critical design practice and its concerns. It brings examples of practice and literature on the practice together in order to provide an account and contextualization of critical design practice that should be of use to any student of product and industrial design and its related fields. It should also be of use to design scholars interested in problematizing critical design practice, be it either as a piece to critique or to employ as an analytical tool in observing the practice. Above all, I hope that the history, the theory, the methods, and examples of practice, presented in the following chapters, shed light on the operation of critical design practice and its contribution to product and industrial design in a disciplinary context.

The structure and approach to writing

The book is broken down into three thematic parts: history, theory, and practice. Chapter 2 presents a history of critical design practice, placing critical design today in a historic context. It discusses how the term 'critical design' appeared some twenty years ago in the design research community as a particular approach in interaction design as a field of industrial design. Referring to a longer tradition of critical approaches in industrial design and architecture, it was meant to re-establish alternative views on product and interface design, telling stories about human values and behaviour that were neglected in commercial industrial design practices. Thus, the chapter charts a history of critical design from its roots in Italian Radical Design, Anti Design, and New Design, in the German and Dutch traditions of Conceptual Design as well as in the critical practice of Human Computer Interaction and Interaction Design. The chapter goes on to show how critical design projects carried out today are heavily influenced by the methods and approaches developed in these preceding practices as well as the anti-capitalist, anti-commercial, ethically led, and activist ideologies that informed these earlier modes of critical practice. Additionally, comparisons of historic and contemporary examples of critical design practice will show how the design language and themes in some critical design practice today mirror, or are at least informed by, work produced over forty years ago. The discussion in this chapter reveals that contrary to the popular understanding of critical design practice, critical design is not such a new or emerging field or movement, but is part of a long and diverse trajectory of critical practice in industrial design and its forerunners have influenced mainstream industrial design practice and theory today.

Chapter 3 begins to tackle the theory informing, and developed through, critical design practice. This chapter aims to illustrate design activity, theoretical perspectives, and methods used in critical design practice. The chapter begins by introducing the theoretical perspectives that inform critical design through a discussion on 'Para-functionality', 'Post-optimal design', and the 'Aesthetics of use' as concepts that have been developed over the past fifteen years to explain how critical design practice works.

The chapter outlines how critical design is perceived as a form of design research. However, it shows how critical design as a research method is not objective or explanatory, and how it is criticized for not being scientifically rigorous because of the inherent uncertainty to be found in the design process and the objects it produces. Critical design embraces subjectivity, ambiguity, and the object as an evocative agent. In short, critical design as a research method sets out to ask more questions than it aims to answer.

With this in mind, the discussion on design activity, theoretical perspectives, and the methods used shows how in a changing territory of design research, critical design practice operates though its provocative objects with ambiguous characteristics. This use of purposeful ambiguity allows the user to see and experience phenomena that would otherwise go unnoticed, as it provokes new ways of thinking about the world through objects. The discussion will illustrate how the open-ended and relational characteristic of critical design is being embraced by disciplines external to industrial design e.g. how critical designers are working with scientists to probe and question difficult ethical sociotechnical questions through the production of objects and scenarios. The chapter contextualizes critical design practice's use in relation to the sciences and the social sciences through a discussion on design examples and methods.

Continuing this inquiry into the theory associated with critical design practice, Chapter 4 considers criticism and function in critical design. This chapter focuses on critical design as a specific field of industrial design practice. It considers barriers to critical design practice being seen as part of a disciplinary project. The chapter begins by arguing that analysis of critical design practice often comes from perspectives developed in art and visual culture. The chapter aims to identify the limitations of analysing the practice from these perspectives. It argues the need for a more design-centric focus. The chapter goes on to discuss how 'function' is used as a concept to ground criticism of critical design practice and to categorize critical design as a form of conceptual art. The discussion shows that 'function' offers insufficient grounds for criticism and categorization. It renders claims that critical design is not design because the objects do not function in a utilitarian sense redundant. Function as a concept is explored to show that an object's function not only has the potential to extend beyond utility, efficiency, and optimization, but even in the strictest modernist sense of the concept, function has always comprised characteristics that move into post-optimal realms, beyond efficient use, utility, and practical specifications. The chapter argues for a relational, dynamic characteristic of function that supports seeing and discusses critical design practice as other examples of orthodox industrial design and not conceptual art. The chapter ultimately locates critical design in its disciplinary context. Building on this, the chapter distinguishes what differentiates critical design from other forms of critical creative practices. It states what is distinct about critical design that primarily relates to how critical design uses the ubiquitous language of product design and narratives of everyday use to engage broad audiences in debate and critique.

Through the presentation and discussion of design examples, Chapter 5 explores what critical design practice is critical of. This chapter presents three distinct approaches to critical practice; these three types of practice characterize contemporary critical design and are defined as associative design, speculative design, and critical design. Drawing from the discussion outlined throughout the book, Chapter 5 describes how associative design emerged from political forms of radical and anti-design, drawing on mechanisms of subversion and experimentation in conceptual art. The critique focuses on disciplinary concerns. Speculative design advances product design to comment on emerging science and technology, drawing on socioscientific research and theories. The critique focuses on scientific and technological concerns. Finally, critical design functions as a form of critical language and offers a sociocultural critique. The chapter establishes how these three approaches in critical practice function as a form of satiric design, in each case the designers use satire in their design work to establish critique and engage user audiences in debate on and around the work through the use of humour. The discussion shows that the characteristics of satire and the range of techniques used to offer a satiric response are appropriate mechanisms to differentiate these types of critical practice. The examples and approaches discussed throughout the chapter identify precise points inherent to the critical attitude in industrial design. Ultimately, the chapter shows that contemporary critical design is a rich and diverse activity engaging with a range of themes, or what are termed throughout the book as matters of concern, where the products and practices of industrial design are mobilized to engage diverse communities and publics in debate about issues pertinent to the design discipline, scientific and technical developments, and sociocultural concerns. Chapter 5 concludes by presenting a taxonomy of critical design practice. The taxonomy incorporates theory, methods, and tactics identified and discussed throughout the book and provides contextual tools and theoretical apparatus to engage with critical design practice. The taxonomy serves as a tool to analyse examples of critical practice and its application is illustrated. The taxonomy also serves as a tool to inform the operation of critical practice and identifies methodological and critical approaches that are of interest to design practitioners and students of design.

In Chapter 6, the book concludes by describing the disciplinary contribution that critical design makes. It discusses the constructive relationship between critical design practice and mainstream design practice. It argues how critical design practice extends the scope and agency of today's industrial designer into new contexts of operation and engagement and how this creates new opportunities for today's product and industrial designers.

The book places critical design practice in a context of product and industrial design practice. It places critical design practice in historic context and discusses the theoretical contexts that designers draw from and position the work in. It discusses the contexts engendered in the design work, the focus of critique, and subjects of investigation undertaken through critical design practice. It discusses where and in what contexts critical design operates, discussing how and by what methods and tactics critical designers operate. With these things considered, the following chapters ultimately serve to contextualize critical design practice and its contribution as a form of practice.

2
HISTORY

This chapter charts a history of critical design practice. It shows that contrary to the popular understanding of critical design, critical design practice is not a new or emerging field, but is part of a long and diverse trajectory of critical practice in product and industrial design. The discussion explores critical design from its roots in Italian radical design, anti-design, new design, and conceptual design – in the German and Dutch traditions – before exploring critical practice in interaction design. The chapter shows how critical design projects carried out today are heavily influenced by the methods and approaches developed through a tradition of critical design practice that first emerged over fifty years ago. A number of comparisons are drawn between historic and contemporary examples to illustrate how the design languages, strategies used, and themes engaged in critical design practice today draw upon a trajectory of critical practice. The chapter discusses the socioeconomic conditions that give rise to critical design practice, and how economic hardship and the academic institution provide contexts that foster and inspire critical practice. What follows aims to place critical design practice today in a historic context.

A forgotten history of critical design practice

Any quick Google search or a more in-depth literature review of critical design practice will undoubtedly first lead you to examples associated with the *Royal College of Art* (RCA) in London in the late 1990s. Until recently, research specifically focusing on critical design made little reference to its rich and diverse history that exists in product and industrial design. In the essay 'Critical design – forgotten history or paradigm shift', Cilla Robach (2005) identified the omission of historical accounts of the practice as one of the most pressing questions facing critical design. Stating how it is difficult to pinpoint where critical design began, Robach writes 'critical design was not new to the 1990s, predecessors can be found in radical and anti-design' and, 'some argue that critical design started with the design collective Droog in their 1993 Milan exhibition, while others suggest it started with Dunne and Raby at the RCA' (Robach 2005, 34). These have all contributed towards the development of a critical design practice that is rich and diverse and are all equally important in the formation of contemporary critical design practice.

An emerging critical design practice

Conceptual and critical forms of industrial design have roots in artistic avant-garde practices, with the earliest form of critical design practice developed in Italy during the late 1950s. This movement has been described in a number of ways and termed 'radical design', 'anti-design', and 'counter design'. Critical design practice has been reviewed in this context by Sparke (2014) and Rossi (2013); these authors address Robach's claims of forgotten history. The focus in their accounts aims to put the contemporary understanding of critical design into a broader historic disciplinary context. Each demonstrates how in Italy, designers began to question orthodoxy and dogmatic approaches in practice in a way that lays the foundation for critical design practice today.

In her analysis, Sparke demonstrates how critical design – as it is popularly understood – has become shorthand to represent critical practice in product and industrial design. She does this by using critical design to retrospectively discuss Italian anti-, radical, and counter design in a form of practice she describes as Italian critical design.

> In essence, the term, which became widely used in the early 2000s and is therefore being used retrospectively in this context, refers to the events, happenings, writings, images and designs created in Italy in the period in question that set out to challenge the cult of the industrially manufactured object, which by the mid-1960s had become the norm. Critical design questioned, and sought to provide an alternative to, the model of ideal, universally valid design that had been promoted by the 1920s international modern movement in architecture and design and, in Italy, by its interwar equivalent, rationalism, and that continued, albeit in a reconstituted form, in the neo-modern Italian design movement of the years 1945 to 1965. (Sparke 2014, 114)

Sparke offers a comprehensive account of Italian critical design that is valuable to anyone interested in the history of critical practice. In essence, Italian critical design established a movement in product and industrial design where the designer's function moved from being driven by that of servicing industry and commercial gain, towards a more meaningfully engaged practice focused on discursive and propositional ends. This form of practice was orientated to critically engage the concerns of the day. It is important to discuss the key moments in this early period of critical design in order to delineate the precedents of contemporary critical design practices and to identify the practitioners, the support structures, and contexts that gave rise to critical design practice.

Challenging hegemony

In Italy during the Linea Italiana, also known as the Bel Design era (1956–1970),[1] product designers for the first time disassociated themselves from the interests of monetary gain and embraced broader political goals, seeking a critical discourse with capitalist consumer society. Here a provocative design culture emerged out of dissatisfaction with the role of designer solely serving production and consumption. In a move from orthodoxy, Italian radical designers attempted to create new and unusual experiences with objects by using ready-mades from industrial production and incorporating them into the designs of furniture and lighting. This approach moved product design beyond traditional notions of functionality to embed intellectual value in the work. Looking for materials suitable to make commentary, the designers promoted emotional play and symbolism over practical function and refuted assumptions of utilitarianism and consumption (Lees-Maffei and Fallan 2014, 53).

Achille and Pier Giacomo Castiglioni were pioneering Italian designers in this area and could arguably be considered the first critical designers. The Castiglioni brothers were successful commercial product designers; however, in an experimental turn, they started to integrate re-definitions of context and use into their product design. They moved away from formal development towards a ready-made ad hoc approach in their design work. The design of the *Sella Stool with Bicycle Saddle* (1957) exemplifies this approach and the divergence from the orthodox design of the day. The stool implies new combinations and ways of using existing things through which the Castiglionis aimed to endow the product with an individual object character. The results were objects that were familiar in form but had a de-familiarizing effect that encouraged the user to interpret the object and its use.

At a similar time, an element of discontent about the function of industrial and product design was voiced in the UK's design education system. Through the 1960s, the noted design educator Norman Potter mounted a critique of industrial design carried out for the purpose of financial gain and cultural exploitation. Potter was part of a group of tutors mostly from the *Royal College of Art* in London who established an experimental design school called *The Construction School* in Bristol (UK) in 1964. In its formative years, the aim of the 'Bristol Experiment' – as Potter refers to the design school – was to set about re-examining certain assumptions of the modern movement in design (Potter 2002, 166). It was established, in part, as a response to the work of many notable educational institutions of the day, including The RCA, Hornsey

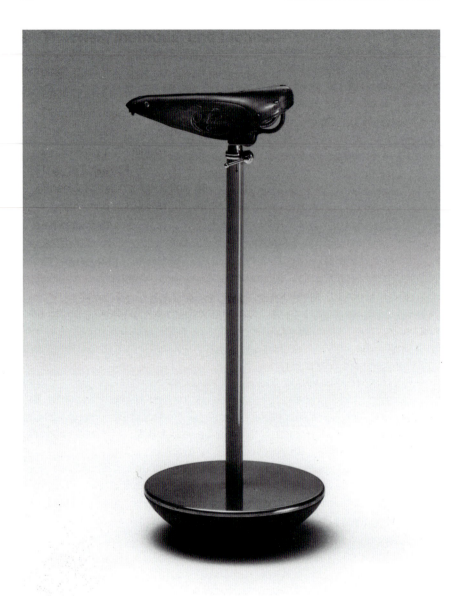

Figure 2.1 Achille and Pier Giacomo Castiglioni, *Sella Stool with Bicycle Saddle*, 1957, production Zanotta 1983. SELLSA seat, design Achille and Pier Giacomo Castiglioni in 1957, production Zanotta 1983. Courtesy of Achille Castiglioni Foundation.

College of Art in London, and the *Hochschule für Gestaltung College of Design at Ulm*. All were experimenting with different aspects of problem-solving disciplines and with systematic design method. Ulm was an influential German design school that built on the modernist ideals of the *Bauhaus*. It believed there should be a reduction to essentials and that functional form should clear society of bourgeois content and steer utilization towards predefined behaviours in use. Its teaching also advocated an objective and socially aware design for industry pioneered by Tomas Maldonado whose teaching defined a role for the designer in a process of social change through design (Maldonado 1972). In the development of *The Construction School*, Potter advocated a more open interpretation of design and its principles; the school was explicit in its political ideology, as can be seen from Potter's writing in the school prospectus, 'our position is ranged-left and open ended', 'putting things together that make sense', and importantly, 'design is a field of concern, response and enquiry as often as a decision of consequence' (Potter 2002, 168).

Anti-design

By the late 1960s, modernism had hit an intellectual standstill. Across Europe, anti-design ideologies were taking hold and a number of design collectives emerged. The collectives formed out of the disillusionment with modernist ideals that had dominated design since the early 1900s. Rather than view design as a benign force, anti-design collectives saw industrial design as having aggravated social and environmental problems. Originating in Italy, anti-design established a tradition of artistic and political discourse in design. Groups such as Superstudio, Archizoom Associati (both founded in Florence in 1966), Gruppo Strum (founded in Turin in 1966), Gruppo 9999 (founded in 1967 in Florence by Giorgio Birelli, Carlo Caldini, Fabrizio Fiumi, and Paolo Galli), Gruppo G14 (launched in the late 1960s by Gianfranco Fachetti, Umberto Orsoni, Gianni Pareschi, Guiseppe Pensotti, and Roberto Ubaldi), and Archigram (formed in the 1960s in the UK by Peter Cook, Warren Chalk, Ron Herron, Dennis Crompton, Michael Webb, and David Greene at the Architectural Association) each shared the desire to critique the world of consumption. Most of the projects developed by these collectives remained as prototypes without ever being mass-produced.

A number of factors facilitated the movement. Most notable were the economic conditions of the time. There was little work available for designers, so they occupied themselves in other ways leading to experimental practices critical of prevailing disciplinary and commercial orthodoxy. The broader air of protest and political activism prominent during the 1960s also had an influence on creative practice and design culture.

Academia supported and fostered critical thought and practice. The relationship between critical design collectives at the time and the academic institution is important to note. In the UK, *The Construction School* provided an environment for critical voice, thought, and practice. In Italy, *The University of Florence School of Architecture* – which educated product and industrial designers – was key in the creation of the early Italian critical design movement, fuelling both its academic staff and students to establish the collectives with the support of the institution.

While linked to academia, the Italian critical designers sought to engage more broadly than the academy, aiming to engage the professional and commercial contexts of design and the design culture of the day. Anti-design projects aimed to open an intellectual discourse through design. The collectives established explicit ideological and intellectual positions, where protest was seen as essential and the work was grounded in direct political action. Rather than design positioned as being in service to problems, design was used to facilitate active participation through happenings, interventions, exhibitions, and publications. The designers aimed to engage consumers in shaping and questioning forms of consumption, community, and industrial models of production at large.

Such an active, concerned, and participatory design philosophy was a common element within anti-design collectives. This model of design was used as a means of communication and political instrument geared to provoke debate on and around the work. The work became a vehicle of critical social theory and produced symbolic new ways of rethinking design as a form of conceptual research. While object-orientated form was applied provisionally to communicate ideas and provoke debate, the projects were ultimately designed for ideological consumption. The work produced criticized and exposed contradictions of a bourgeois society born out of a functionalist ideology, which was limited to driving consumption through mythologies of optimization, utility, and practicality in use and product styling. In the majority of cases, projects lost practical-functional connotations and acquired symbolic, cultural, and existential functions – these types of 'function' in critical design are discussed at length in Chapter 4.

One of the key protagonists in the Italian critical design movement was Ettore Sottsass who began to exhibit his critical design objects in the mid-1960s. Sparke writes

> Sottsass challenged the supremacy of the mass-manufactured cult object through the very activity of designing objects. Two key means of challenging neo-modernism in Italian design preoccupied Sottsass. The first related to his discovery of a whole new meaning for the object, associated with ritual and spirituality. Among the many artefacts he created in response to that visit he designed a number of small ceramic objects that deployed India-inspired imagery and that, he claimed, contained the message that 'love and attention can take the place of manipulation and use' and proposed 'a formal re-invention of objects simply through the mediation of the eastern figurative world'. The second was linked to pop culture during a trip to the United States. While the first helped him to understand how objects could perform a deconditioning function as much as a conditioning one (that is, they could liberate as much as they could enslave), the second offered a new meaning for the designed object that was innocent, spontaneous and, in his view, ideologically untainted. (Sparke 2014, 126)

An influential critical design group at this time was Alchimia. Alchimia used mundane designed objects to proclaim trivial culture as the new high culture. They implemented this approach through the reinterpretation of design classics by adorning them with paintings and ornaments or by elevating the status of everyday objects through provocative and performative acts.

Critical design was journal dependent and as Sparke (2014) describes, Casabella magazine in the 1970s was a principle medium for the dissemination and exposure of projects. Mendini was Casabella's editor between 1970 and 1975 and was key in the development of critical design practice as a contributor to Studio Alchimia and Casabella. Mendini provides us with an early example of where the critical designer took on the role of editor, curating and publishing work and images for forms of cultural consumption in the magazine. A noted example of this approach is Mendini's *Lassù (Up There)* performance (1975) in

Figure 2.2 Alessandro Mendini, Destruction of Lassù chair, 1974. © CSAC – Universita Degustudi di Parma/Arch. Alessandro Mendini, Milano.

which he burnt an archetypical chair proclaiming a new age in design through the symbolic destruction of the most familiar of objects and the object that 'every designer aspires to design'.

In 1973, Casabella assisted in the formation of Global Tools, a free school for the development of individual creativity that offered opportunities for discussion. Global Tools was an experimental programme of design education founded by the members of the Radical Design movement including Sottsass and Andrea Branzi, among others. It was conceived as a diffuse system of laboratories firstly in Florence, Milan, and Naples and with the support of the design media, it aimed to establish an alternative relationship with the Italian design industry.

Between 1973 and 1975, the design and architecture collective Superstudio belonged to Global Tools. Superstudio was at the heart of Italian critical design. Pessimistic about politics, the group developed visionary scenarios in the form of photomontages, sketches, collages, storyboards, films, and exhibitions of a new anti-design culture in which everyone is given a sparse, but functional, space to live free from superfluous objects. As we will see later in the chapter, Superstudio's politics, concerns, and communication strategies resonate today amongst contemporary critical design practices.

In 1972, concepts from Italian radical and anti-design were presented in *Italy: The New Domestic Landscape*, an exhibition held at the Museum of Modern Art, New York. Curated by Emilio Ambasz, the exhibition showcased examples of Italian design that drove Bel Design, but included the design provocateurs who pioneered an alternative and critical practice. Ultimately, mainstream design culture consumed the provocative designs. Journals and magazines written and edited by designers for designers had very little reach beyond design culture. The objects and images of Italian critical design found their way into the high design/art galleries of the 1980s and in such the political, critical, and anti-consumerist grounding was somewhat diluted (Julier 2000, 78). Nevertheless, these practitioners initiated an international reorientation in product and industrial design and for a time managed to overcome the doctrine of practical functionalism, optimization, efficiency, and commercial orientation that arguably still governs product and industrial design practice. This period from 1959 to 1972 introduced a wave of critical, socially, and politically engaged designers that expanded the disciplinary purview of industrial design and established a role for designers beyond that of an agent driving capital though the production of manufactured goods.

Participatory design

While in Italy anti-design collectives aimed to engage participation through happenings, objects, and interactions presented in galleries and through publication, another form of participatory design was emerging in Scandinavia that was equally critical of hegemony and which advocated a new approach within industrial design practice.

Participatory design, as it was to become known, is a practice that attempts to involve actively all stakeholders (e.g. employees, partners, customers, citizens, end users) in the design process to help ensure the design work meets their needs. It enhances the agency of the user in the design process by having them actively cooperate with the designer. Participatory design focuses on processes and procedures of design and is not a design style but a process. This approach has a political dimension of user empowerment and democratization. Participatory design emerged in the late 1960s, born out of ideas of democratizing the workplace and ideals of cooperation and collaboration in design. It explores design as a collaborative practice and prioritizes the design user as a key stakeholder. It emphasizes the tacit knowledge of the participant and the design process's ability to elicit and externalize this knowledge through the interaction with design objects, playful interactions, and stages exercises carried out in co-design workshops (Muller, Wildman, and White 1993). One of the guiding principles in participatory design is to expect controversy rather than consensus within the process. Founded on the principle of creating legitimate participation for all stakeholders during periods of technological change, participatory design explicitly engages with ethical issues in social intervention. The aim of participatory design is to engage the imagination of participants rather than merely see them as respondents in a design process or as agents to observe and generate data from (Schuler and Namioka 1993). The premise for this approach, in practice, was that the stakeholders using the design – be it product or service, environment, or policy – are best informed of their needs. Therefore, these stakeholders should be brought into the design process to participate actively in the designing. Today, participatory design methods are integrated into mainstream design practice. However, in its formative years, the notion of participation on the part of the user in an authoritative design process was radical. It challenged the professional role of the designer and the role of the design process. In effect, within participatory design practice, the designer's role moved from that of styling or innovating tangible and physical products and systems to act as John Thackara would come to describe as the facilitator of large groups of people (Thackara 2005, 7). In this context, the designer needed to develop the methods and processes of design in order to achieve the types of conditions required to activate and facilitate interactions between users and stakeholder groups.

Like critical design practice, participatory design reflects critically upon the relationship between the designer and the communities that are being designed for, and, or with. These practices operate beyond conditions set by fiscal gain or technological development and are established as intellectual and politically motivated practices, and increasingly extend designs agency as they are used to inform policy in address to societal concerns.

Unikat Design: Adding nothing but the concept

In the 1980s, a German counterpoint to market-led design emerged. Setting itself apart from the German tradition of 'good form' and functionalism, the Neues Deutsches Design (New German Design), sometimes referred to as Unikat Design, aimed to instigate a public debate through alternative design methods and through a revival of the ad hoc approaches pioneered by the Castiglioni brothers. Informed by the postmodern turn in design, driven by the Italian radicals, but also affected by seminal publications such and *Charles Jenks and Nathan Sliver's Adhocism: The Case for Improvisation* (1972), objects made from trivial materials and waste products were created in small series, or as one off unique design pieces. This recombination of material and object components implied a critique of consumer culture, playfully subverting disciplinary norms and political conditions of the day. Collectives, such as Stiletto, used everyday objects from beyond domestic space and transformed them into furniture. For example, Frank Schreiner's *Consumer Rest Chair* was designed as a satire of the retail experience. *Tarantula* by Schulz-Pilath was designed to look like a spider crawling through the living room. The group Kunstflug combined nature and artificiality in floor lamps that took the form of trees offering a counterpoint to good form, while Herbert Jakob Weinand embedded narratives of the Cold War within the design of the *Pershing table*, which through its form satirized the nuclear tensions of the day.

Starting from a similar aesthetic position, offering a critique of consumer culture but also engaging discourses of environmental sustainability and reuse, Droog design was established by critic Renny Ramakers and jewellery designer Gijs Bakker in the early 1990s. Droog pulled together a number of like-minded young furniture designers from the Netherlands. Droog's first cohort of designers mostly came from *Design Academy Eindhoven*. Here again we see the importance of the academic institution facilitating critical practice. The Eindhoven approach was to focus design as social commentary considering a larger cultural agenda. Like in the Italian and German traditions, Droog had taken an antiauthoritarian spirit, an interest in the vernacular. They translated these interests into design work that had the quality of collage. Despite the ad hoc appearance of the work, Droog's early pieces suggested formality and integrity, a strong sense of proportion, and legibility. In its formative years, Droog designers saw their task as gathering objects on the streets and reusing them, combining design work with a strong sense of irony. Droog's ethos was not to add new forms or ideas; indeed the collective, as Ramakers (2002) states, suggested they should reuse those as well. The result was objects such as Tejo Remi's *You Can't Lay Down Your Memories: Chest of Drawers* (1991), which is traditional in its shape and operation but made of various pieces of discarded furniture. In Remy's drawers, since neither the type of object nor material was new, the familiar reassembled in a new manner that was stronger. The radical nature of Droog's ethos is further represented by Richard Hutten's bench design *S[h]it on it* (1994). Shaped as a swastika, the bench is a literal, although ironic, example of the object as an expression of ideology.

Figure 2.3 Tejo Remi, *You Can't Lay Down Your Memories: Chest of Drawers*, 1991. © Tejo Remi/Hans van der Mars.

New German Design groups and Droog represented a renewed confidence in critical and conceptual design that first appeared in Italy some thirty years earlier. The aim of these was not to manufacture industrial products, but to provide a critical examination of consumer practice in the political and sociotechnical concerns of the day. These include attempts to use juxtaposition and caricature, unusual materials and suggestions for alternative ways of using things, and living with objects, in order to create awareness of the designed objects, the effects of consumption, and the impact that design might have on the world, but also to employ product and industrial design as a medium for commentary.

Representative design

During the 1980s, product designers practising in a technological and electronically orientated context began to recognize the potential challenges faced by the industrial designer as electronics were increasingly integrated into all sorts of domestic products. At this time, industrial designers were primarily 'skinning' or housing electronics, with little input into the design of the electronics and design of the interactions that would inevitably arise from growth in electronic and digital products. In a critique of dogmatic industrial design approaches to designing the electronic digital product, Daniel Weil argued that designers were ill equipped to satisfy the demands placed by the digital product and developments in interaction design. Wiel offered a critique of how designers were treating electronic products in his *Radio in a Bag* (1981), which consisted of transistor radio components in a printed plastic bag. The design parodied how designers were treating electronic product design at the time by literally packaging the components but at the same time introducing transparency. Wiel went on to teach at the Royal College of Art and while there wrote:

> Industrial design must set about a re-interpretation of the languages and values – the mind set – of the mechanical and electronic world. This is not only because the new technologies demand the capacity for a broader and more abstract approach, but because of the emergence of such challenges to the established order as environmental awareness and major geopolitical changes. This requires the reassessment of design, production and marketing throughout the industrial chain. Therefore, we must give more intellectual depth to the experience of designing. To meet future challenges, the profession must recapture its traditional cultural and strategic brief. A brief that requires the translation of cultural values into contemporary ideas and products. It will not be enough to provide competent technical or problem solving services. (Wiel 1994, 123)

Weil placed emphasis on a shift in design education by endorsing a design culture that embraces intellectual experiment through design. He outlined a design process of 'interpretation, representation, and communication' (Wiel 1994, 120). A representative form of design subsequently emerged from the RCA's Industrial Design department during the late 1980s and early 1990s. This practice was born out of concern with the uncritical appropriation of the digital electronics. The designs produced at the RCA at this time exploited a new freedom that digital technologies offered.

Similarly, students on Cranbrook Academy of Art's Industrial Design course in Detroit, USA were exploring the potential of product semantics. The design work was pursued through linguistic semiotic theory, aiming to understand the structure of language and how it conveys meaning and translating semiotic theory into product design. Many of the objects produced explored visual languages for information technology, hardware, and consumer electronics. They used metaphors to establish relations between objects and culture, aiming to move the designer closer to their audiences. Julier writes:

> it must be remembered that the Cranbrook approach was working as an educational laboratory for ideas, that while its proposals did much to challenge the hitherto accepted norms in design language, in the so called 'real world' its products would probably only appeal to niche markets. (Julier 2000, 102)

Julier's commentary can be extended to the RCA's representational approach. The activity on both sides of the Atlantic was ultimately orientated around existing archetypes, for example redesigning phones, televisions, and personal computers. With this focus, it sustained dominant design and technological ideologies i.e. more of the same differentiated by simple semantic styling exercises. The designs would not penetrate the market because of excessive production costs and, as Dunne (1998, 26) argues, fell short of their provocative potential because of the commercial focus on semiotic functionality.

Designing interactions

From the mid-1990s, themes of ubiquity and the integration of the digital into domestic objects had driven experimental work developed at institutions such as MIT's Media Lab, Xerox PARC, and companies such as Philips (A Telier 2011). Projects carried out within these institutions aimed to process and lead redefinitions of technology and the design of technological products. The intention was to develop and problematize digital communication technologies and human interaction with them. The integration of digital technologies into product design was informed by thinking in Human Computer Interaction (HCI).

Arguably, it was the marriage of HCI and emerging approaches in product design, which created the field of interaction design.

Interaction design brought together information scientists, psychologists, designers, and computer specialists to develop the interface between human and computers. Gillian Crampton Smith, William Gaver, Anthony Dunne, Phoebe Sengers, and Phil Agre were amongst some early designers associated to this move in critical design practice. By challenging hegemonic notions of interaction and human object relations, there have been various attempts within Interaction Design – and its contributing disciplines – to develop critical terms that inform contemporary design practice. For example, 'critical computing' is the topic of a small decennial conference exploring issues of society, democracy, and ethics in systems development. The goals of this community in 'taking critical action' have been effectively integrated into development methods and processes, for example in participatory design (Muller, Wildman and White 1993) and in reframing certain disciplines such as informatics. Philip Agre (1997) and Floyd (2005) outline an approach they term 'critical technical practice' that applies critical theory for analysing historical and operational frameworks in the field of artificial intelligence. While not explicitly addressing notions of criticality, these approaches in HCI have argued for increased reflection in practice. For example, Jonas Löwgren and Erik Stolterman (2007) argue for developing thoughtfulness about personal design ability as a question of assuming responsibility for one's professional activity and design thinking. Phoebe Sengers has developed a model of reflective practice as a means for both designers and users to rethink dominant metaphors and values in HCI (Sengers 2005; Sengers, McCarthy, and Dourish 2006). Developing a model of 'design for reflection', Lars Hällnas and Johan Redström have led foundations for exposing design issues in what they term the 'the aesthetics of use' as an approach that indicates commitment to reflection within design practice, upon design effects, and in use (Hällnas and Redström 2002a).

Somewhat laying the path through this terrain, under the direction of Gillian Crampton Smith, the Royal College of Arts Computer Related Design (CRD) studio set out an agenda for product and interaction design, positioning it as a vehicle for critical reflection on the role of design and technology in society (Crampton Smith 1997). The programme specifically explored ways that the traditional skills and knowledge of art and design disciplines can be applied to the design of new technology, artefacts, and systems. The focus was on interactive media, intelligent objects, and responsive environments (Crampton Smith 1994; Crampton Smith and Tabor 1996). Extending the representational approach developed in the Industrial Design department and research in HCI and interaction design, the 'Critical Design' unit was established within the Computer Related Design Studio led by research fellows Anthony Dunne and Fiona Raby.

Critical design at the Royal College of Art

So as a term 'critical design' originates from the RCA, appearing some twenty years ago in the design research community as a particular approach in human computer interaction. It describes a method of working that the Computer Related Design Studio used in a number of projects between 1994 and 2005. Referring to the longer tradition of critical approaches in industrial design and architecture, it aimed to re-establish alternative views on product and interface design, telling stories about human values and behaviours that were neglected in commercial industrial design practices. We first see the term 'critical design' introduced by Gaver and Dunne in the paper *The Pillow: Artist Designers in the Digital Age* (1997). In the paper, they discuss the role of artist designer and present a design-centred methodology in which hypotheses and ideas are explored through design. They propose design activity aimed not towards realizing marketable products for industry, but instead towards challenging ideas for the public about user's relationship with objects. Rather than being centred on needs and problem-solving, they suggest product design can and should be about ideas and provocation. Gaver and Dunne's introduction explains how critical design employs methods that are associated with fine art practice. However, in understanding the difficulty in extending product design's agency in this way, they identify the attributes that make the critical design objects of design rather than objects of conceptual art. They do this with reference to *The Pillow* (1995) designed by Dunne as part of *Hertzian Tales* (1994–1997)

The Pillow is an abstract radio used to encourage awareness of the local electro-climate. It picks up mobile phones, pagers, walkie-talkies, and baby monitoring devices. It questions notions of privacy as although the person listening to conversations is a social invader, the radiation from the phone call is invading their home and body.

Gaver and Dunne (1997, 361) draw attention to the physical design and the material qualities of the object, characterizing it as product design by the use of inexpensive components and construction techniques characteristic of mass-produced objects.

The design was initially shown as part of the *Monitor as Material* exhibition (1996). The ambiguous design of the object proved problematic. In the gallery space, the experience of seeing the design is separated from everyday concerns and as a result, the design required explanation. Addressing this, Dunne developed an extrinsic narrative – or scenario of use – in the form of a pseudo-documentary. The documentary titled *Pillow Talk* features a user interacting with the object. This exercise situates the object in a context of use. The documentary supports the assertion that *The Pillow* is an object of design because the user audience can see the design in context and hear the user

Figure 2.4 Anthony Dunne, *Pillow Talk* documentary still, 1995. The Pillow (documentary still) video: Dan Sellars.

describe their interaction with it. The assertion that the object is a prototype design encourages the viewer to consider it in an everyday context of use. This prompts the viewer to ask different questions of the object than if it was treated as an artwork or an outcome of some other creative practice – this difference will be further discussed in Chapter 4.

Since critical design's popularization, the term has come to represent almost any form of design practice attempting to establish a critical move through design. In some respects, this has had a detrimental effect because it has not been representative of the diversity in examples of critical design practice nor is it inclusive of the rich history of critical design practices that preceded it. However, as this chapter suggests, this is changing with the increasing popularity of the practice and with increased design writing exploring contemporary critical design – for example in Sparke's retrospective account of Italian critical design. Furthermore, increased analysis of the practice and its linage, for example Mazé (2007), Malpass (2012), and Rossi (2013), have worked to contextualize critical design within the disciplinary canon and shed light on its influence. The rest of this chapter moves to explore the influence of examples of early critical design on examples that are more recent. It shows synergies that exist between the tactics employed and themes addressed through practice.

Synergies between precedent and contemporary examples of critical design

In the essay 'Where is the designer on identity and plurality', Scholz (1989) presents a range of examples demonstrating the main intentions of the design approaches taken in the work of the Italian critical designers, New German designers, and Droog. Scholz introduces a number of salient tactics employed in practice that are useful when analysing critical design.

Describing the critical designers use of obsolete objects, Scholz introduces the concept 'context transfer' to describe when one object is taken out of context and placed into another to give new meaning and function, exemplified in the case of the Castiglioni's *Sella Stool*. She uses the term 'cut up' to describe new combinations of materials and collages that could include historical elements exemplified in Droog's and Remi's *You Can't Lay Down Your Memories*. Finally, she talks of 'hybrids' in which contrary to the traditional concept of homogeny in design, trivial objects are changed through the addition of extrinsic elements as exemplified through many of the strategies employed by Superstudio and Archigram (Brandes, Stich, and Wender 2009, 41). These methods work to establish the critical move through a narrative and object typology that offers a form of material commentary. These approaches are common in contemporary examples of critical design practice and demonstrate the synergies between examples of critical design developed at different points in its history.

Superstudio and Archigram used objects and collage in the production of magazine publications to visualize localized utopian futures. The legacy of their design language, approaches, and the narratives that were constructed through technocratic visualizations, storyboard illustration, and photomontage to build scenarios is commonly applied today. We can see a clear example of this methodological lineage if we compare Archigram's *Instant City Airships* (1968) by Peter Cook alongside Brendan Walker's *Chromo 11: Airlife Seat Belts* (2004).

Instant City Airships proposes a mobile technological event that drifts into underdeveloped, drab towns via air (balloons) with provisional structures and performance spaces in tow. The effect is a deliberate overstimulation to produce mass culture, with an embrace of advertising aesthetics. The event is intended to eventually move on, leaving behind advanced technology and cultural hook-ups.

Chromo 11: Engineering the Thrill draws inspiration from the traditions of the fairground methods of the French Situationists. The proposal aims to design new types of stimulating thrilling experiences. *Airlife* from Chromo 11 is a collection of thrill rides based on the fusion of the European Airbus A340 and the English

Figure 2.5 *Instant City Airships, The Airship in Lancashire*: Model/collage, Peter Cook, © Archigram 1970.

Figure 2.6 *Chromo 11: Airlife Seat Belts* 2004. © Brendan Walker; 2005; *Thrilling Designs: Chromo 11* Volume Two; Aerial Publishing, London.

home. Walker's use of photomontage resonates with the techniques and visualizations used by Superstudio and Archigram. The comparison of scenarios demonstrates synergies between the early critical design collective and Walker.

A similar comparison can be drawn between Superstudio and Dunne and Raby. Superstudio's *Il Monumento Continuo* (1969) proposed a gridded superstructure that would wrap around the world. Eventually, this structure would cover the entire surface of the planet leaving a featureless urban environment that inhabitants would plug into to meet their living needs. The point was exaggerated but poignant: Superstudio was commenting on the way globalization and consumption was dominating society. Taking this to a logical extreme, the collective proposed a future society living in a large anonymous megastructure in a networked existence. The proposition is even more poignant in retrospect when considering Superstudio proposed the scenario in a pre-Internet era and long before any discourse relating to an 'Internet of Things'.

In *United Micro Kingdoms* (2013), Dunne and Raby propose a noir technological future. In one scenario, they introduce a section of society that they call Digitarians. Digitarians 'depend on digital technology and all its implicit

Figure 2.7 Superstudio (Frassinelli, Magris Alessandro e Roberto, Toraldo di Digitale (1)(A). Francia, Natalini): Supersurface, *The Happy Island*, project 1971. New York, Museum of Modern Art (MoMA). Ink, airbrush, graphite, and cut-and-pasted printed paper on paper 19¾× 27⅝" (50.2 × 70.2 cm). Given anonymously Acc. n.: 1254.1974 © 2016. Digitalimage, The Museum of Modern Art, New York/Scala, Florence.

totalitarianism – tagging, metrics, total surveillance, tracking, data logging, and 100 per cent transparency'. Their society is organized entirely by market forces; citizen and consumer are the same. For them, nature is there to be used up as necessary. They are governed by technocrats or algorithms – no one is entirely sure, or even cares – as long as everything runs smoothly and people are presented with choices, even if illusionary (Dunne and Raby 2014).

Synergies can be drawn between these two examples of critical practice, both in terms of the medium and the style in communication. The use of collage or photomontage to establish the visions of a future is present in both examples; this offers a hyper-real stylized aesthetic that aids in affording the dilemma of interpretation, because at the same time the scenario is both seductive and jarring.

Moreover, the themes engaged through practice resonate with each other even though they are operating fifty years apart; both practices challenge technocracy, the influence of globalization, and the effect of technological consumption, automation, and networks. Each speculates on the effect of these on sociotechnical futures and both propose uncanny trajectories of progression.

Figure 2.8 Dunne and Raby, *United Micro Kingdoms*: Digiland, 2013. CGI: Tommaso Lanza.

Recent examples of conceptual furniture design by Martino Gamper, Marti Guixe, and Studio Ball apply mechanisms in practice that reference the work of Droog and New German Design, and ultimately approaches of cut up and context transfer pioneered by Achille and Pier Giacomo Castiglioni.

Figure 2.9 Martino Gamper, Olympia from the series *100 Chairs in 100 Days,* 2005–2007.

These comparisons serve to illustrate that critical design has a rich history in practice and that tactics, themes, and approaches have developed over time.

Conclusion

The primary aim of this chapter is to contextualize critical design as part of an older tradition of criticality in product and industrial design. In charting this brief history, the discussion shows how the term 'critical design' appeared some twenty years ago in the design research community as a particular approach to human computer interaction. However, as part of a longer tradition of critical approaches in product design, it was meant to re-establish alternative views on product design, telling stories about human values and behaviour that were neglected in commercial product design.

The chapter identified social and technological conditions that led to the emergence of critical practices. A salient observation is how examples of critical practice emerge out of turbulent political, economic, and technological shifts. Whether it was the disillusionment with functionalism, the political turmoil of the 1960s, or the technological shift from the mechanical to the digital paradigm, designers active at these times find their voice through design practice.

In many of the examples discussed, we see how critical design practice is rooted within an established community of practice supported by institutional contexts. The Art School has historically supported the practice and the role of the educational institution is significantly important. The educational institution facilitated the 'Bristol Experiment', the University of Florence facilitated Italian anti-design, the Cranbrook Academy experimented in product semantics, and Eindhoven supported Droog. Furthermore, The RCA and the Computer Related Design Studio provided environments for experimentation with new technology and approaches to designing that would not be carried out in an applied industrial context. Although this is historically significant, it pertains to contemporary practice. As we will see in later chapters, the majority of critical design practice carried out today is associated with academic institutions and is often framed as research carried out within this context.

Paradoxically, the structures and media that contribute to and support commercial and professional design culture; publications and exhibitions, for example, also support critical design practice, since work is disseminated through galleries and the popular design press. Here we see a problem in critical design practice in that it is dependent on its links with the design culture within which it operates and simultaneously critiques.

Critical design projects carried out today are influenced by the methods and approaches developed in earlier examples of practice. They are influenced by the anti-capitalist, anti-commercial, ethically led, and activist ideologies that informed earlier modes of critical practice. The discussion shows how contemporary examples of critical design practice are informed by aesthetic principles found in older examples. The benefit of looking at the history of critical design practice comes from identifying design methods used to establish the critical move through design. This short review of precedents identified 'cut up', 'context transfer', 'hybridity', and 'technocratic visualization' as methods used to build ambiguity into objects to achieve defamiliarizing effect that provokes the user to engage in meaning making and provokes thought through the object's design. These methods are used today in contemporary examples of practice to establish the critical move and position design as a field of concern. Positioning design as a field of concern, response, and as a mode of inquiry is a fundamental principle that grounds contemporary critical design practice. Here design practice and its objects facilitate a way of knowing, exploring, projecting, and activating the relationship between users, objects, and the systems that they exist in. The following chapter explores in detail the theoretical and methodological approaches in practice that afford such a function in critical design practice.

3
THEORIES, METHODS, AND TACTICS

This chapter aims to illustrate design activity, theoretical perspectives, methods, and tactics used in critical design practice. It introduces these perspectives initially through a discussion on *para-functionality*, *post-optimal design*, and the *aesthetics of use.* These concepts are used to explain how critical design practice operates as a medium for inquiry. It discusses how critical design functions as a form of design research, arguing that the practice is not objective or explanatory, but instead focuses on intersubjectivity and proposition, posited through the act of product design. In this context, the purposive function of the design work is discursive where the designer aims to generate debate about the themes engaged in the design work. The chapter shows how the open-ended and relational characteristic of work produced by critical designers is embraced by disciplines external to product design. The chapter contextualizes critical design practice's use in relation to the sciences and the social sciences, before starting to discuss the contribution that critical design practice makes to the product and industrial design discipline. The chapter ultimately places critical design in a theoretical and disciplinary context.

Design as a medium for inquiry

Critical design practice is used as a medium to engage user audiences and provoke debate. It does this by encouraging its audiences to think critically about themes engendered in the design work. Operating in this way, critical design can be described as an *affective*, rather than an *explanatory*, practice in so much as it opens lines of inquiry as opposed to providing answers or solutions to questions or design problems. Mazé and Redström (2007) describe this function by explaining that the practice is not aimed at simplification, but diversification of the ways in which we might understand design problems and ideas. The focus here is on the epistemic qualities of the designed object i.e. how objects encourage us to think in tangible ways when we consider how they feature in everyday life. Applied in this way, the design of objects – and the scenarios that they exist in – can be employed to create a descriptive comprehension of complex issues.

Sarah Gold's *Alternet* (2014) offers a good example of this. The *Alternet* explores the complex and pressing issue of data privacy through the proposition of an 'Alternative Internet' infrastructure that is community-owned, and where the retention of ownership of personal data is paramount. It counters hegemonies that surround Internet and data usage in an age dominated by optimism surrounding the Internet of Things, and the benefits of cloud computing and big data driven by the big four: Microsoft, Apple, Facebook, and Amazon. People are now aware of the manipulation and profiling made possible by the huge amount of data we all produce when using information technologies. The services that constitute the Internet depend on our data sustaining their businesses. In this scenario, recovering control of our privacy means regaining control of our data. The *Alternet* is a fair trade, radically reinterpreted Internet structure that provides data ownership through straightforward data licences and open-source hardware and software that are used to establish an autonomous mesh network reliant on a sense of civic duty. It allows individuals to choose whether to share their data and how their data is used. Users become participants as the *Alternet* is established and stewarded by the Alternet Co-operative, its users. In this way, the Alternet differentiates itself from the Internet and darknets because it is a digital commons – a civic alternative. Gold's work presents an alternative for communications by proposing the products, infrastructure, and the service system required for the *Alternet* to function. It interrogates questions around transparency of data ownership. In doing this, it makes visible complex concerns in relation to how personal data is used and private information commoditized. The design of the hardware, software, and contextualizing material that Gold presents draws attention to this issue through familiar form and expectations of use. As a long-distance mesh network, the Alternet grows organically with each new router that is added. The router cases are made on a standard desktop 3D printer. The cases are designed to prevent malicious nodes from being added to the network. Each router is printed with a fingerprint that is unique and verifiable against a public database of router IDs, so any compromised router is automatically removed from the network until the community are able to assess it. In addition, the routers are made with special catches that mean to adapt the router requires the printed box to be physically broken, acting as a visual warning that the router has been compromised. These security solutions are designed to make it 'just hard enough' to deter people from maliciously adopting the network. A data barometer accessed through a smartphone application makes an invisible material visible and actionable. Each time an individual opens their Alternet operating system, they see their barometer that displays a colour diagnostic that changes colour depending on the last service to request the individual's data.

The approach resonates with storytelling, but this is a form of storytelling through object, service, and systems design. This makes the narrative accessible and compelling. The design makes the issue tangible and engaging.

Used as a medium of inquiry, product and industrial design increases the understanding of an issue through the user engagement and discussion that takes place around the design object. This engagement provides opportunities for critical design as a form of inquiry because it opens discussion and ultimately new insights can be gained from this discussion. This tactic is grounded in an understanding that user audiences naturally understand the world through material form, and through interaction with objects. This understanding and expectation of use is leveraged through the introduction of communicative objects that provoke discussion. This use of critical design facilitates a way of knowing, exploring, projecting, and understanding the relationship between users, objects, and the systems that they exist in. Through debate and interaction, critical design objects enable us to consider matters more immediately than abstract theories.

Figure 3.1 Sarah Gold, *The Alternet*, 2014. Alternet Community Network Kit/photo by Lynton Pepper/license: CC-BY.

Post-optimal design and para-functionality

The most notable project that introduces these tactics is *Hertzian Tales* (Dunne 1998). In *Hertzian Tales*, Dunne introduces a form of design practice that operates outside technical and commercially driven product design. Dunne frames product design as an investigative medium to stimulate debate. This position is established through a critique of mainstream product design and the Human Factors community's preoccupation with technical function in the design of electronic products.[1] Dunne argues the need for design practitioners to reconsider the ambition to create a tight fit between user and product. He defines this move from efficiency and optimization as 'post-optimal':

> The most difficult challenges for designers of electronic products now lie not in technical and semiotic functionality, where optimal levels of performance are already attainable, but in the realms of metaphysics, poetry and aesthetics where little research has been carried out. (22)

In this approach, objects of design are positioned to draw attention to unseen conditions in everyday life. Dunne aimed to engage users to consider dominant technological development and practices of use. In *Hertzian Tales*, he does this through five design proposals that figuratively interact with the electromagnetic landscape. In the example of the *Faraday Chair* (1997), the furniture provides shelter from electromagnetic fields invading homes. It is a utilitarian shelter providing refuge from the constant bombardment of telecommunication and electronic radiation. In essence, the object draws attention to an invisible and crowded electromagnetic landscape in the domestic context. It asks questions about the implications of this penetrating and leaking electronic radiation, for example, what information is being transmitted, who owns this electromagnetic space, and what are its impacts, etc. Ultimately, the project exposes part of our material and technological culture that normally goes without consideration and is unquestioned in everyday life.

The *Faraday Chair* is an example of a post-optimal object. This object functions through a type of use that Dunne terms 'para-functionality':

> a form of design where function is used to encourage reflection on how electronic products condition our behaviour. The prefix 'para-' suggests that such design is within the realms of utility but attempts to go beyond conventional definitions of functionalism to include the poetic. (39)

Figure 3.2 Dunne and Raby, *Faraday Chair*, 1997/photograph: Lubna Hammoud.

Through the post-optimal object, product design is employed to more propositional ends, an approach that slows the interaction and forces interpretation of the object's use. This suggests a subversion termed 'user-unfriendliness':

> If user-friendliness characterizes the relationship between the user and the optimal object, user-unfriendliness then, a form of gentle provocation, could characterize the post-optimal object. The emphasis shifts from optimizing the fit between people and electronic objects though transparent communication, to providing aesthetic experiences through the electronic objects themselves. (32)

Through practice and writing on critical design, Dunne and Raby establish a dichotomy between critical design and mainstream design (Dunne 1998; Dunne and Raby 2001; Dunne and Raby 2014). Here conventions within industrial and product design orthodoxy are set against conventions in a critical practice, i.e. optimal against post-optimal, functional against para-functional, and user-friendliness against user-unfriendliness. This position is useful in understanding and studying critical design practice in how it offers a theoretical anchor from which to question critical design's position in relation to an orthodox product and industrial design practice.

Dunne explicitly characterizes critical design in opposition to affirmative design (1998, 68). In this model, affirmative design reinforces predominant social, technical, or economic values, whereas Dunne and Raby's critical design strives for an alternative form of product design, positioned as a medium for inquiry.

> Design can be described as falling into two very broad categories: affirmative design and critical design. The former reinforces how things are now; it conforms to the cultural, social, technical and economic expectation. Most design falls into this category. The latter rejects how things are now as being the only possibility, it provides a critique of the prevailing situation through designs that embody alternative social, cultural, technical or economic values ... Critical design, or design that asks carefully crafted questions and makes us think, is just as difficult and just as important as design that solves problems or find answers. (Dunne and Raby 2001, 58)

Fundamentally, this approach is positioned as a form of social research that integrates aesthetic experience with everyday life through conceptual products. The approach goes beyond product optimization and uses estrangement to open the space between user and object to provoke discussion and criticism. Through this, the narrative possibilities offered by designed objects and how these narratives might afford forms of engagement with objects and the designer's commentary are explored.

Like Dunne and Raby, Robach characterizes critical design as being in opposition to affirmative design, describing how it rarely offers solutions to the problems:

> Where the modernist design paradigm was imbued by the conviction that there was an objective, true and good solution to all problems, conceptual design emphasizes problems' complexity. (Robach 2005, 35)

In essence, critical design does not offer practical solutions to everyday problems; instead, it seeks to meet peoples' emotional and intellectual needs:

> a type of design that does not continually strive to make our lives easier, but rather trouble us an annoyance with the aiming to make us look critically at our lives and society in general. (Robach 2005, 36)

Robach argues that critical design pushes disciplinary boundaries, increases awareness, and transgresses limits of orthodox product design. In its role as provocateur, our prejudices as users are revealed and boundaries become fluid or frayed. In her commentary, she draws attention to the element of social criticism in critical design, stating however that 'this criticism is not partisan if it is directed at big social problems such as consumption and production' (Robach 2005, 36).

There are, however, some issues with this affirmative/critical dichotomy. Its formulation is open to interpretation and political consideration rather than useful in identifying and understanding examples of practice. Its grounding is based on value judgments. The reality is that distinctions between critical and affirmative forms of design are not as clear-cut as this manifesto might depict. In working to understand the practice, there is a need for a broader vocabulary and analytical framework that captures nuances and the spectrum of approaches.

The poetic mechanisms first detailed in *Hertzian Tales* are used to establish the designer's critical position and aim at stimulating the user's imagination through interaction. They emphasize the importance of narrative and storytelling in the development of critical design work. However, these interactions are not afforded through the actual use of the design object, but through strategies of rhetorical use.

Rhetorical use

Rhetorical use in critical practice is established by constructing narratives of use. This means designing the object's context and the presentation of scenarios that give meaning to the object. This is often achieved with media that is external to and situates the design object. Typically, this takes the form of film, images, photomontage, and vignette. In establishing narratives of use, the designer takes on the role of a storyteller and author where fictional scenarios are developed to position the object, but also where the imagined or rhetorical interaction with the object itself works to make the fictional scenarios believable. As we saw in the example of *The Pillow* in Chapter 2, the ambiguous objects that characterize critical design practice are made sense of through material that situates the work in an everyday and familiar context. The object and contextualizing material taken together can be defined as a design device.

Through rhetorical use, critical design practice aims to explore what might be and to establish alternatives that offer an experience similar to the quality of poetic language. This encourages the user to imagine the object in their lives, while simultaneously creating a dilemma of interpretation within the user. This dilemma of interpretation encourages the user to question the qualities of the object and the narrative of use that contextualize it. It is within this dilemma of interpretation, and in the suspension of disbelief, that questions can be asked of the product design and of the designer's critical position.

Discursive design

Post-optimal design, para-functional objects, and rhetorical use are used to establish the designed object as a form of discourse. In practice, discourses allow for a certain way of seeing, understanding, and commenting. Here the use of discourse is not limited to disciplinary or linguistic discourse but entire ways of understanding things, where one knows through discourse, as discourse allows for the production of certain and individual truths. In critical design, the act of designing – including the subjective interpretations and processes that inform the work – is established as a mode of discourse[2] and so critical design is close to what Krippendorff describes as 'designing the design discourse' (Krippendorff 2006, 32). In designing the discourse, critical design practice can be described as a form of critical thought amongst other forms of critical thinking. Bruce and Stephanie Tharp describe this intention and role in practice:

> The primary intent of the discursive designer is to encourage users' reflections upon, or engagements with, a particular discourse; the goal is to affect the intellect. As distinct from objects of art, architecture, and graphics, which can all be agents of discourse, products have particular qualities that offer unique communicative advantages. (Tharp and Tharp, 2009)

Examples of discursive design include Diller + Scofindio's *The Vice/Virtue glass series* (1997) produced for the exhibition *Glassmanifest*, in Leerdam, the Netherlands. In the design of drinking glasses, each glass in the series – Dispensary (blown glass with a compartment for Prozac), Exhaust (blown glass with a cigarette), and Fountain (blown glass with integrated hypodermic needle) – serves one addiction. Though the work, the designers explore contradictory cultural attitudes towards addiction and health, where the hacked glasses accommodate the dual pursuits of health and hedonism.

The Near Future Laboratory designers', Julian Bleecker and Nicolas Nova, *Slow Messenger* (2009) offers another example of discursive commentary through design intervention and playful experiment. Through the design of the world's slowest instant messenger, the designers explore how in a digitally networked era contact is perpetual and ubiquitous. The device delivers a message through a deliberately primitive text display that turns the torrent into a trickle and the user has to wait for the message to reveal. Implemented as hardware, it uses a 96×64 pixel display; the design questions how our connectivity often results in meaningless communiqués and dispatches.

Another example of discursive design is Superflux's *Open Informant* (2013). *Open Informant* takes the form of a networked object including a phone app and e-ink badge. The app searches your communications for National Security Agency trigger words and then sends text fragments containing these words to the badge worn by the user for public display. Using the body as an instrument for protest, the badge becomes a means of rendering our own voice visible in an otherwise faceless technological panopticon. By openly displaying what is currently taken by forceful stealth, Superflux questions the intrusive forms of surveillance adopted by democratic nations on their own citizenry. Through the design, they aim to shift the discussion around wearables from being about you and your body as machine to the culture of machine intelligence and algorithmic monitoring.

The aesthetics of use and meaningful presence

Lars Hällnas and Johan Redström have developed an approach in interaction design that is interested in engagement rather than error-free optimized performance. They argue that to optimize practical functionality with respect to utilitarian perspectives is not enough in the design of objects and interactions (2001, 2002a, 2002b). Aesthetics with its rich framework for critique may be used to extend the scope of product design by critically examining it from within practice (Redström 2008). They extend the concept of the post-optimal object and the aesthetic experiences it aims to afford, through the concepts of 'aesthetics of use' and 'meaningful presence'. They argue that aesthetics is the proper foundation for technology design as it turns from its focus on efficient use towards concerns for what they call 'meaningful presence' (Hällnas and Redström 2002a, 108). Meaningful presence challenges the design and evaluation of an object in relation to a definition of what the object is, towards a focus on what the object may mean.

> In human-computer interaction, we usually think of the computer as a tool for achieving certain ends, such as creating a document or searching for information. We thus evaluate the usability of computational artifacts in relation to criteria such as efficiency, simplicity of use, and ease of learning, based on relatively precise descriptions of what they are used for. We may call descriptions of things along these lines functional descriptions based on a general notion of use. This is what we do when we ask what a house, or a hammer, is and answer with a description telling what houses and hammers in general are used for. (Hällnas and Redström 2002b, 107)

These functional descriptions of objects focus on objectives of use without reference to the person using them. However, definitions of use can be described in other ways that relate to a particular meaning given to an object. This is described as the presence of an object. Presence is defined in terms of how the object expresses itself when the user encounters it:

> When we ask a friend about a certain piece of furniture in her home and she answers that it is the table she got from her late grandfather. Clearly, it would

be inappropriate to answer such a question with 'it is a piece of furniture on which you can put this or that kind of object provided it does not weigh more than X kg'. When we ask questions about this particular table, we do not ask for its general use, but about its existence in our friend's life, its role or place. When we learn what it is, we get an existential description of what this particular table is to our friend, a description based on the table's presence in her life. (Hällnas and Redström 2002b, 107–108)

Such a perspective considers objects as bearers of expressions rather than functions. This constructivist perspective aligns with Krippendorff's (2006) thesis on designing that states that users construct situated meaning when they encounter objects – a perspective grounded on ecological cognitive theory, radical biological constructivism and Wittgenstein's notion of 'language games'. For Krippendorff, designers should employ second-order understanding in designing if the artefacts are to be useful, usable, and understandable by users. In other words, when designers can anticipate the meanings users will assign to an artefact during use, then they might successfully represent the user perspective in the design process (Krippendorff 2006).

However, where Krippendorff suggests that the user might be understood, Hällnas and Redström, like Dunne and more recently Wilkie (2010), outline the complexity in trying to understand the user through empirical observations based on need and efficient use.[3] They argue that designers cannot anticipate the meaning users will assign to an artefact during use, and therefore, to represent a generalized user in the design process is at best a tentative aim (Dunne 1998; Dunne and Raby 2001; Hällnas and Redström 2002a).

As Redström (2006) points out, the subject has become more important than the object in much of design and design research. The 'subject' who emerges from user-centred design, however, is not a 'humanist' subject; he or she is an 'engineered' subject, who responds correctly to stimuli and thus can be shaped into a reliable member of mass society, whether conceived on consumerist or social-progressive grounds. Dunne and Raby challenge this conception of the user:

This enslavement is not, strictly speaking, to machines, or to the people who build and own them, but to the conceptual models, values, and systems of thought the machines embody. User-friendliness helps to naturalize electronic objects and the values they embody. (Dunne and Raby 2001, 30)

Users are messy, complex, and unpredictable. By embracing the unpredictability in how a user may interact with an object, there is a need to observe a richer relation to our things, for example, through the exploration of engagement rather than efficiency in use and through alternative forms of use that fundamentally challenge expectations of use and the user.

Advocating such agency, Flusser (1999) argues that designers should shift their agenda and see objects as bearers of expression rife with intersubjective qualities. Such a focus will deliver design that is more meaningful.

The focus on intersubjectivity and expression is a fundamental concern in critical design practice. Shifting focus beyond efficient use to embrace uncertainty, expression, interpretation, and meaning – in order to deliver a critical point of view – offers a complementary perspective to dominant thinking and applications in product design practice.

This shift in focus has important disciplinary implications; first, the potential for critical design practice to establish critical distance between object and human subject through poetic techniques of aesthetic, fiction, de-familiarization, and estrangement allows us to deepen our understanding of product design through a reflective disciplinary practice. This shift in focus from use to meaning adds to the disciplinary understandings of what functional objects are and can be. This in turn contributes to a culture of design that is more considered and thoughtful about its actions and impacts.

Second, a shift in focus towards intersubjectivity and expression ultimately has the potential to increase the agency of product design and its breadth of focus. In a reflexive and critical practice, the function of product design shifts from problem solving to exploratory problem-finding contexts. An indicator of this extended agency can be seen in how critical design practice is increasingly embraced for its exploratory potential, and its challenging and sometimes activist agendas by disciplines considered external to product and industrial design.

Exploratory potential

There are a growing number of projects and collaborations between science, the social sciences, and critical design practice. Communities from the sciences and social sciences are looking to critical design practice and see potential for its application in an ambivalent zone between emerging science and material culture. In a merging of the design studio and laboratory, these projects aim to foster and exploit post-optimal practice. In this context, a critical and somewhat speculative design practice is used to question the potential applications and implications of scientific and technological theories and research being carried out today and how these developments might manifest in future.

A notable example of critical practice applied in this context is *Impact* (2009). As a project, *Impact* placed Royal College of Art designers with Engineering and Physical Science Research Council UK (EPSRC) scientists, technologists, and engineers. The collaborations aimed to provoke user audiences to consider the importance of engineering and the physical sciences and research that is being carried out; it comprised sixteen mixed-media critical and speculative design research projects. The research topics ranged from renewable energy devices and security technologies to synthetic biology and quantum computing. The project was considered by EPSRC to offer powerful insight into how today's research might transform our experience of the world (REF 2014).

Alive: Designing with the Materials of Life (2013) highlighted designers interacting with emerging science with a particular focus on biological fabrication. The exhibition, held in Paris curated by French designer Carole Collet, showed the work of thirty-four designers engaging themes of synthetic biology and nature as a model to design by. Collet's 2012 project Bio-lace is representative of the projects exhibited. In her practice, Collet investigates the intersection of synthetic biology and textile design to propose future fabrication processes for textiles, utilizing design fiction to communicate the science. In *Biolace*, Collet proposes to use synthetic biology as an engineering technology to reprogram plants into multipurpose factories. In a series of four scenarios, plants are genetically engineered to produce textiles at the same time as food. For example, a tomato plant with high levels of a nutrient called lycopene that could help improve the skin's resistance to sunburn and protein-rich edible lace growing from its roots, and a basil plant that could produce anti-viral medicines as well as perfumed lace for use in decorative fashion applications. A strawberry bush with black lace growing from its roots would yield black strawberries enriched with enhanced levels of vitamin C and antioxidants, while a spinach plant could produce microbiological sensors for use in electronics at the same time as providing a multimineral food supplement. The scenarios are communicated through a design device consisting of four images of the plants depicting the fruit and by-product and an animation that contextualizes the speculation. The aim of this project is to bring to light the potential of emerging living technologies and to question the pros and cons of extreme genetic engineering and biofacture – manufacturing with living technologies.

In a similar context, *Big Data: Designing with the Materials of Life* (2014), supported by The Medical Research Council, Clinical Sciences Centre, UK, provided a platform for designers to work with emerging scientific theories and thinking in relation to how big data is informing scientific practice. The project was carried out in a live and public design studio at Central Saint Martins, University of the Arts London (UAL). It explored the growing challenges of processing, editing, and storing large amounts of digital data. Designers from the MA Textile Futures Programme (Central Saint Martins, UAL) and architects from the Interactive Architecture Lab (RC3, the Bartlett School of Architecture, University College London) transformed ideas from big data into blueprints for design futures for perceptible dissemination to the public.

This territory is becoming increasingly populated with examples. Activity at this intersection of design and science is emerging as common practice in critical and

Figure 3.3 Strawberry Noir, part of the *Biolace* series, © Carole Collet 2012.

speculative design. For example, designer Daisy Ginsberg's *Synthetic Aesthetics* provides a wealth of examples of design engaging synthetic biology (Ginsberg et al. 2014). Nelly Ben Hayoun's practice includes a number of projects that involve public engagement with science and technology, ranging from exploring themes of particle physics, space travel, and asteroid apocalypse. Ben Hayoun is noted for her collaborations with NASA Ames Research Centre and the Seti Institute (search for extraterrestrial intelligence) to develop product design film and performances to engage publics in scientific discourse through speculation. Recently, the European art-science programme has supported this mode of practice where *Studio Lab – Blueprints for the Unknown* (2016) provides a catalogue of projects delivered by studios and designers synonymous with the critical and speculative design canon engaging developing theory and thinking in scientific and technological contexts.

In this design/science context, critical design practice is a useful medium to test sociocultural embargos that might exist towards realizing the application and domestication of new science and technologies. It is applied to open debate around the science in affective rather than explanatory terms. This affective function offers a complementary perspective to that of science, which is arguably focused on facts and answers rather than fictions and provocative speculations.

Design fiction

Design fiction is closely related to critical design practice. However, it is better seen as a method or tactic rather than a field of practice. Design fiction brings together approaches from product design, science fact, and science fiction. This combination of practices challenges the expectations of what each does on its own and ties them together into something new. Design fiction speculates about new ideas through prototyping and storytelling, where the design device functions like props or conversation pieces that help users imagine. Design fictions are important because they afford us the ability to see the world not only how it is, but also as it could be. It is a way of materializing ideas and speculations without the pragmatic restraints of commercial product design.

Design fiction utilizes what Kirby (2010) describes as the 'diegetic prototype'. Diegetic prototypes depict future technologies in terms of need, viability, and benevolence to large public audiences. A science or technology that only exists in the fictional world is called diegesis. These objects have form and are grounded in scientific reason and potentially feasible technologies but only exist in a context of rhetorical use and in the imagination of the user. Julian Bleecker of the Near Future Laboratory describes how design fiction functions in this context and is reliant in the users' imagination to complete the design proposition: 'Artefacts become real through the activities of the agents who engage in the task of giving the artefact meaning proper to the idiom in which the agent operates' (2004, 5).

The decisive factor in design fiction is the ability to see the world not only how it is, but also as it could be. A familiar theme runs through many examples of design fiction; the focus is on challenging the status quo, the subversion of orthodoxy, the criticism of the obvious, and the proposition of an alternative. Design fiction is utilized to develop new realities and review them with concrete images and objects, products and interfaces, characters and spaces, and collections and scenarios. Design fiction emphasizes the real and fictional, the evident, possible, unexpected, and imaginary. It looks to science fiction as a storytelling genre that creates prototypes of alternative worlds, other experiences, and other contexts for everyday life, all based on the creative insights of the designer. It is positioned as a practice that embraces the character of science fiction and storytelling and challenges essentialist views inherent in design and science practice. Bleecker writes, 'As much as science facts tell you what is and is not possible, design fiction understands that constraints are infinitely malleable' (Bleecker 2010, 63). Design fiction is regularly used in speculative and projective forms of critical design practice.

The Design Fiction group at MIT applies design fiction to explore novel ways to spread debate using social/viral media and popular culture; a number of projects exemplify the approach. *(Im)possible Baby* (2015) by Ai Hasegawa, Sputniko!, Asako Makimura, and Moriga focuses on biotechnologies that could enable same-sex couples to have their own, genetically related children. Though the fiction, they propose that delivering a baby from same-sex parents is not a sci-fi dream anymore, due to developments in genetics and stem cell research. In this project, the DNA data of a lesbian couple was analysed by 23andme (a biotechnology company that offers personal genome services) to simulate and visualize their potential children. The team then created a set of fictional, future family photos using this information to produce a hardcover album that was presented to the couple as a gift. To achieve a public outreach, the team worked with the Japanese national television service, NHK, to create a 30-minute documentary film following the whole process, which aired in October 2015.

Tobias Revell's *New Mumbai* (2012) is another example of the use of design fiction. Revell developed a pseudo-documentary that appeared to document the Dharavi slums of Mumbai, India, showcasing how genetically modified mushrooms have revitalized the poverty-stricken city in the 'New Mumbai' of the future. The documentary tell the story of how a highly experimental biotechnological sample had been stolen from an Amsterdam laboratory, where the fungi had been re-engineered to exponentially grow in size for use as narcotics and to create a micro-economy based off the material. As the new plant became introduced into the overpopulated but highly educated urban mass of the slums, the locals began to use it to their advantage – to both exercise freedom from the state and to provide suitable living conditions. The narrative details how today the mushroom is used to harvest energy as well as to provide heat, light, and building material for the residents of the slums of Dharavi. Revell's documentary creates a super-fiction that extrapolates from emerging scientific work and places it in contexts that are derived from the observation of geopolitical trends. The technology is situated in context through a first-person account of users who have interacted with the technology: the scientists, the lawmakers, and those living in the future slums. The documentary has a familiar and almost mundane quality in its narrative and production. This is successful in making the fiction all the more believable.

Speculation and proposition

Speculation and proposition is a central tactic in critical design practice. The approach is most apparent in speculative design. Speculative design as a specific form of critical design practice focuses on socioscientific and sociotechnical concerns. Speculative design is discussed in Chapter 5 as an independent category of critical design practice. It is important to introduce it here because of its specific focus and theoretical grounding.

A common approach in the techno-centric domain of product design is for the designer and technologist to focus on what technology can do and to often ignore the contextual factors. Speculative designers specifically address the contextual issues that can turn a technology into a product, and in turn modify the human experience of that technology. Speculative design asks why we should adopt emerging technology and science, and what are the potential implications if we do?

Speculative design functions in two ways; first as a practice, it looks at advances in science and technology and proposes them in domestic settings. Through the creation of tangible prototypes, it is possible to project the existence of emerging technology and scientific developments into a near-future context. Second, it is a form of practice that is used to reimagine the technological present. Speculative design is not concerned with dominant trends in technological progression but the variety of possible technologies and paths of progression that we choose.

James Auger has developed significant work that defines speculative critical design through practice and writing. Since 2001, The Auger-Loizeau design studio, led by James Auger and Jimmy Loizeau, has produced a body of speculative design work engaging themes of robotics, cybernetics, telepresence, connexity, and microbiological fuel development. Auger's thesis *Why Robot* (2012) provides a practice-led account of how speculative design operates and functions as a form of research through design. The approach within speculative critical design that domesticates emerging science is demonstrated through Auger-Loizeau's *Happylife* (2009), a project that questions what it would mean when an electronic device knows more about a family member's emotional state than you do. Demonstrating how the affective function of critical practice is valued by experts in the field of science and technology, and more importantly their funding bodies, *Happylife* is the result of a collaboration with the Computer Science Department at Aberystwyth University in the UK involving Reyer Zwiggelaar and Bashar Al-Rjoub's Engineering and Physical Sciences Research Council (UK)-funded research that looks at real-time dynamic passive profiling techniques and the ubiquitous monitoring of a person's emotional state. By reading changes in physiology, *Happylife* communicates the user's emotional state and can predict changes in emotional state. The designers built a visual display linked to the thermal image camera that acts like an emotional barometer, one for each member of the family. The project speculates about if the science was introduced into the home and how might it be used in everyday life. It questions if we would constantly want our emotive state read and communicated to our family? It probes the interactions and potential conflicts that might occur around the science, questioning the value and application of the technology in a quotidian setting. It once again makes developments in science tangible and familiar with the aim of engaging broader communities of interest.

In speculative design, designers take scientists and engineers as active collaborators in understanding how specialized components of practiced science and engineering knowledge, in their local contexts, can be configured into broader and informed approaches to living in a complex world. This rationale leads to immersive experiences mediated through interaction with objects, ultimately questioning when technology becomes too invasive in everyday life.

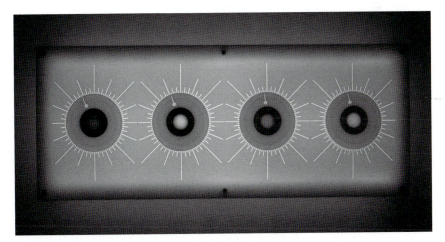

Figure 3.4 Auger-Loizeau, Happylife family display 2009. © James Auger. Auger-Loizeau, *Happylife*, 2009.

Speculative critical design is analogous to writing, focusing on materializing abstract technology. Many examples are similar to the works of Gromala, Hayles, Bruce Sterling, and William Gibson[4] who, as writers, analyse the circumstances within which designed artefacts are made and integrate and implicate culture with stories that Crisp (2009) describes as adding substance and value to design function in the way of all good critical writing. Crisp describes this type of author as a *Designwright*:

> Designwrights examine, evaluate and elucidate practices, cultural forces and artefacts. The characters and events they imagine into being often use unorthodox means, which is in part the power of the work. The delivery handily bellows, where convention would only mumble. (Crisp 2009, 106)

Like good science fiction, and authors such as Sterling, speculative designers deliver information, story, place, and voice by way of creative responses to everyday experience, sometimes in hopes of helping change the tide. It is for this reason that it is a form of critical design practice.

Speculative design requires an alternative form of thinking to that of dominant technological and design rationality. These examples take a substantive view of technological progression. In this respect, the work shares similarities with philosophers of science and technology. A notable similarity comes from Andrew Feenberg (1999, 2002) who suggests that choosing between paths of technological progression is essentially a political one and that modern technological advancement is not neutral as it embodies values and ideologies of industrial society. Speculative design makes the choice between these paths of technological progression visible. It is used to identify and probe the values that user audiences hold in relation to scientific and technological progression and to propose alternative value systems to dominant technological ideology, envisioning technological futures based on different sociopolitical values. Here, speculative design enables the user to see and reflect on larger technological contexts and different technological futures that raise questions about existing conditions in the present. This tactic affords the user the insight required to question vectors of technological progression. This approach draws intellectual concepts from scientific theories and embeds them into artefacts and scenarios of use that tell stories, expose truths, and critique current sociotechnical hegemony.

One tactic employed to do this in critical and speculative design is through the development of counterfactuals. Like good movies about time travel and the consequences of changing history, a counterfactual design project offers a narrative in which an event or situation has been changed in the past and a history is developed that establishes an alternative present and depicts an alternative trajectory of socio-technical development. The point here is that our present was shaped by decisions made in the past and emphasizes that future technological progression is dependent on decisions we make now. Sascha Pohflepp's *Golden Institute* presents a good example of the counterfactual in critical and speculative design. The *Golden Institute* is based on an alternate present where Jimmy Carter defeated Ronald Reagan in the 1980 Presidential election. After winning, Carter established the Golden Institute as a research department on the scale of the American Apollo space programme to find ways of integrating climate change mitigation and environmentally friendly energy generation. As a scenario of technological change, the project encourages reflection on the relationship between state, individual, and nature in through narrative and object that portray the fictional agency. For example, in a scenario where cars are used to chase man-made lightning storms to collect energy.

Speculative critical design focuses on how social, political, and cultural values affect scientific research and technological innovation, and how these, in turn, affect society, politics, and culture. Because of this focus, the practice is increasingly informed by sociological theories of Science and Technology Studies (STS), a theoretical tradition with a shared agenda.[5]

Wilkie and Ward (2009) argue that STS provides theoretical and critical insight into the design development and dissemination of issues relating to design and technology. This is matched by how sociologists are discussing the potential convergence of critical and speculative design. The convergence of STS, and the area of speculative and critical design, articulate and materialize issues of concern and contribute to the formation of publics and alternative futures. Speculative and critical design can serve as a resource for supplementing STS's conceptualizations of, and practices towards, public, engagement, and science (Michael 2012). Examples that have come to illustrate this convergence include Tobie Kerridge's work focused on the strategies employed in critical speculative design in order to design debate and engage publics (Kerridge 2015). This portfolio of work takes a critical view of how the technoscientific development of new materials is partitioned from the public. The project reviews roles for product design by engaging a broader public in a discussion on scientific and technological developments. Rather than being satisfied with the claim that the function of critical design is to engage audiences in debate, Kerridge problematizes the notion of debate, and of public engagement, addressing the questions 'who engages with the design?', 'in what contexts?', and 'how is the engagement useful?' – questions that should be asked in any critical speculative design project.

Michael (2012) argues how speculative and critical design can serve as a resource for supplementing STS's conceptualizations of, and practices towards, public engagement with science. An example of this approach can be found in *Material Beliefs* (2009). *Material Beliefs* brought together designers and biomedical engineers to explore how the public relates to scientists behind

Figure 3.5 Sascha Pohflepp *Golden Institute*, 2009.

advancements in bioengineering (Kerridge 2009). The tactics employed act on the many issues surrounding bioengineering technologies and public engagement as an integrating and illuminating force by bringing different people together. Emerging biomedical and cybernetic technology is applied outside of laboratories and visualized in everyday contexts and presented in public spaces including workshops, schools, and music festivals. The project focused on technologies that provide novel configurations of bodies and materials, and how product design as a tool for public engagement can be used to stimulate discussion about the value of these new technologies. Rather than focusing on the outcomes of science and technology, *Material Beliefs* approached scientific research as an unfinished and ongoing set of practices. They challenged the science often happening in laboratories and separate from the public domain.

Within the project, *Neuroscope* by Elio Caccavale in collaboration with Reading University's Cybernetics and Pharmacology department carried out in 2009, proposes a novel relationship between the laboratory and the home by providing an interface for a user to interact with a culture of brain cells that are cared for in a distant laboratory. This product locates complex scientific processes within the home. Additionally, Tobie Kerridge's *Vital Signs* (2009) demonstrates how bodies generate live behaviours in remote products; he shows how body monitoring enables new biomedical applications and links these new technologies to debates about data security and child safety. These examples from *Material Beliefs* normalizes science, domesticating it and, at times, making it seem somewhat mundane in order to make themes accessible to broad audiences. In this way, the design work acts as a boundary object that fosters a more democratic discussion about science and technology. *Material Beliefs* offers a compelling example of how the function of critical and speculative design resides in the boundary object and the formation of publics around the design work in debate, about the themes, topics, and the position taken by the designer or design team.

Constructing publics

Throughout this chapter, critical design practice has been framed as an imaginative authoring practice, a way of describing, materializing, and exploring ideas about the role of objects in a sociomaterial reality and in exploring scientific and technological futures. This practice allows designers and the publics who form around the work to interrogate sociomaterial reality through proposition, exaggeration, and presentation of alternative visions of reality – be these *visions of the future* or *visions of an alternative present*. Critical design practice offers audiences communicative material that reflects, and orchestrates, an array of concerns. When design is used to provoke reflection and discussion on these concerns, one bridges imagination and materialization by modelling, crafting things, and telling stories through objects. These devices effectively become conversation pieces in a real and persuasive sense. Through the projection of design scenarios, design fictions, and narratives of use, the designer as storyteller shifts focus beyond efficient use to embrace uncertainty, interpretation, and meaning.

Objects of critical design practice facilitate a way of knowing, exploring, projecting, and understanding the relationship between users, objects, and the systems in which they exist. Through familiar form objects act to bridge understanding, offering a site for users to bind together around the object from multiple positions, perspectives, levels of expertise, and understanding. This formation of users around the object is described by DiSalvo (2009, 2012) as the construction of a public. It is through the interactions within the constructed public that debate occurs and the system that the design work exists in – either real or fictional – is discussed and challenged. Through the construction of publics that make matters of concern immediate, critical design practice has the ability to increase societal awareness, motivate, and enable action through the design device.

Natalie Jeremijenko's *Feral Dogs* Project (2005) demonstrates how this application of critical design facilitates a democratic discussion about technology and technological policy. *Feral Dogs* consists of hacked robotic toys with integrated environmental sensors so that they behave in particular ways in response to environmental contaminants. *Feral Dogs* is a compelling example of how concerns can be made public and engage a non-expert community in a discussion that they might not otherwise engage with. Through the project, Jeremijenko demonstrates the possibilities of creatively appropriating technology by engaging a public in political issues surrounding science; in this case, monitoring environmental pollution in the Bronx, New York. The dogs are platforms through which to question, contest, and reframe notions of expertise in technology use and environmental monitoring. They challenge perceptions about how science is done, who does it, and how the results of this engagement and activity can generate results that might affect change in a political and environmental context. In this case, how it empowers the community to lobby policy and environmental officials in order to improve conditions in the locality. Here, critical design moves beyond speculation and proposition to serve socially responsive agendas through a form of creative activism.

Ambiguity

Positioning design as an affective medium that aims to construct publics and question hegemony is challenging. The intent to engage an audience to speculate on design in their everyday life and on the developments of new science and technologies moves product design beyond object-centred approaches to specifically situate the object in a broader network of social relations.[6] This 'relational design' perspective is discussed by Blauvelt (2008), who suggests that the participation of the user informs the product and, by extension, the designer's awareness of complex subtleties in complex user behaviours. Critical design practice embraces the relational open-endedness of product design; it reinforces relational qualities through ambiguity and paradox that encourage the user to interpret the object. Therefore, in critical design practice, the design objects are more open-ended because of the ambiguous, fictional, and speculative characteristics that move beyond optimization and efficiency to require some measure of interpretation and imagination on the part of the user. Such a role encourages exploration, reflection, and engagement. Key to establishing this engagement is ambiguity purposefully designed into the work produced through critical design practice.

The use of ambiguity is essential in critical design practice to overcome a conditioned familiarity with design and use. Jean Baudrillard describes how commodities cultivate designs that support the production and consumption that capitalism requires and illustrates a conditioned familiarity. This process keeps dominant design and technological ideology alive that becomes invisible and alienates from the real in such a system that normal objects are taken for granted (Baudrillard 1981). However, when objects are made unusual and ambiguous, what was invisible and lost in the familiarity of the everyday is made visible. Critical design favours ambiguity; anticipation and interpretation are essential in the design work that critical designers produce. The design proposals produced in critical design practice aim to have a defamiliarizing and estranging effect in order to dissociate the users from their normal modes of use. It is the potential of critical design to make things unfamiliar and strange that allows us to start thinking about how we might use and design objects differently. This is significant in engaging a user audience. Moreover, this disassociation provides insight into new experiences and beliefs, and has the potential to generate new knowledge. Ambiguity as a characteristic and estrangement as a method shift concepts of use beyond the practical and efficient use and conditioned routine and interaction to more meaningful interactions. In this context, product design plays an effective role. Furniture designers, Ralph Ball and Maxine Naylor, effectively describe this instrumental use of ambiguity in critical design practice:

Paradoxically, paradox and ambiguity used in the right context can work to reveal and illuminate, and to reconcile opposites in a holistic way. They give shape to overlapping and contradictory issues which pragmatic and pedestrian delivery often fails to achieve. For an idea to really speak as an object, that is, a thing in three dimensions, it must have more than one dimension. (2006, 56)

Here, Ball and Naylor are pointing to dimensions of meaning and association that they describe as 'correspondence and context' (2006, 56), inciting understanding that supplements the more obvious and inescapable physical dimensions of objects. They write of 'selective contradiction' (2006, 56) that can add rich conceptual texture and sensations that stimulate thoughts difficult to define in words. 'Correspondences and context' is similar to Redström and Hällnass's 'meaningful presence' (2002a) in that they aim to move use and function beyond the object towards existential relationships between designer, object, and user where the work becomes a vehicle for an exchange of ideas.

Bill Gaver was among the first to theorize this approach by introducing 'non-rational design' as a form of design that is about evoking, communicating, developing, and instantiating ideas in a form of prototype design that utilizes purposeful ambiguity. Non-rational design rejects idealized notions of design, working towards a new efficient, optimized, and perfect world. Critical design can indeed be considered a form of non-rational design. Gaver, Beaver, and Benford (2003) discuss the opportunities that non-rational design and ambiguity bring when designed into objects. Ambiguity in design impels people to interpret situations for themselves; it encourages the user to start grappling conceptually with objects, systems, and their contexts and thus establishes deeper and more personal relations with the meanings offered.

A playful paradox exists in non-rational design in that non-rational design is absolutely reasoned and designers operating in this context need to be in control of how ambiguity functions in the design work as Gaver stresses, 'ambiguity is not a virtue for its own sake nor should it be used as an excuse for poor design' (2003, 240).

> Ambiguity should not be allowed to interfere with the accomplishment of well-defined tasks, particularly in safety-critical environments. But in the many emerging applications for everyday life, we argue that ambiguity is a resource that designers should neither ignore nor repress. (2003, 233)

> In a commercial practice, product designers work to eliminate ambiguity: their main effort goes into balancing clarity of use (making it intuitive) with richness of semiotic suggestion (making you like what it stands for). Both aspects of the design attempt to control the user's interpretation of the product – that is, to reduce ambiguity. The most important benefit of ambiguity, however, is the ability it gives designers to suggest issues and perspectives for consideration without imposing solutions. (2003, 240)

Gaver, Beaver, and Benford introduce three types of ambiguity that are essential in the operation of critical practice: contextual ambiguity, ambiguity of information, and relational ambiguity. These approaches are useful in analysing how critical and speculative design functions and how critical designers utilize purposeful ambiguity to achieve the desired output in a project.

'Contextual ambiguity' (Gaver, Beaver, and Benford 2003, 236) can question the discourses surrounding objects, allowing people to expand, bridge, or reject them as we see fit. Blocking the interpretation of a product in terms of an established discourse can create an ambiguity of context. This is useful in spurring people to approach a particular system with an open mind, and more generally, to question the assumptions they may hold about the use of objects. Jurgen Bey's Foam Matters: *The Model World Maquette* (2007) offers an example of ambiguity of context the Styrofoam model is presented as the finished design. The material is contextually inappropriate in the construction of furniture. Working at this scale enables Bey to remain on the ideas level, free from logistical restraints.

'Ambiguity of information' (236) impels people to question for themselves the truth of a situation. A number of tactics are used to enhance ambiguity of information. These focus on creating or reflecting uncertainties about information that are noticeable to people. The purpose of this may be merely to make the system seem mysterious or impressionistic, but more importantly it can also compel people to join in the work of making sense of a system and its context. An example of ambiguity of information, Dunne and Raby's *Foragers Part of the Project between Reality and the Impossible* (2010) proposes a future where to

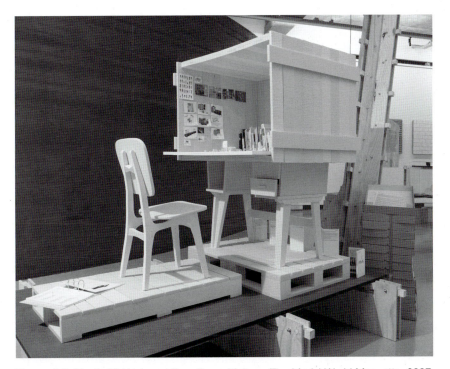

Figure 3.6 Studio Makkink and Bey. Foam Matters: The Model World Maquette, 2007. Photographer: Bob Goedewaagen.

tackle food shortages because of overpopulation through genetic engineering we would need to genetically modify the digestive system in order to take on food that at present we are incapable of processing and forage for foods. Their proposal brings together trends in localized production, activism, guerrilla gardening, and highly controversial scientific developments. In order that the design proposal is accessible, this information is delivered in a detailed synopsis and the objects contextualized by image and film.

Finally, 'Relational ambiguity' (237) can lead people to consider new beliefs and values, and ultimately their own attitudes. It creates the condition for a personal projection of imagination and values onto a design. This allows products and systems to become psychological mirrors for people, allowing them to question their values and activities. As an example of relational ambiguity, Björn Franke's *Traces of an Imaginary Affair* (2006) allows the user to self-harm to feel self-worth. The design relies on the understanding that self-harm is wrong but questions through juxtaposition tension and contradiction how harming can instil value and worth.

In each case, ambiguity frees users to react to designs with scepticism or belief, appropriating systems into their own lives through their interpretations. In the process of reacting to the system, either positively or negatively, users

Figure 3.7 Dunne and Raby, *Foragers Part of the Project between Reality and the Impossible*, 2010. Photographer: Jason Evans.

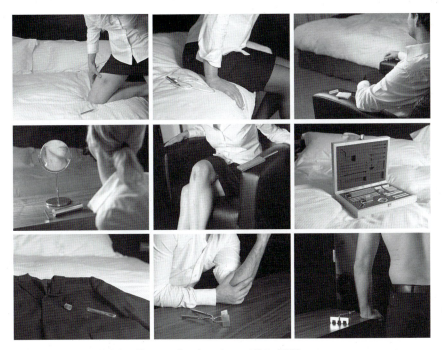

Figure 3.8 Björn Franke, *Traces of an Imaginary Affair*, 2006.

engage with issues that the designer suggests. Therefore, the use of purposeful ambiguity and paradox is a tactic central to critical design practice.

By supporting this balance, ambiguity not only represents a useful resource, but also a powerful sign of respect for users as well. Therefore, although not directly part of the design process, users obtain a strong position in critical design practice. The individual, non-conformist appropriation of objects is most appreciated and encouraged and, as such, the relational and individual meaning-creation is an essential part of the design. We will see later in the book how these three types of ambiguity offer a means to differentiate between contemporary examples of critical design practice.

Satire

Making objects strange and using purposeful ambiguity in address to serious issues create paradox and contradiction and with paradox and contradiction, critical design inevitably appears humorous. Humour is important in critical design practice; projects are often playful, and on occasion seem obscure due to their characteristics and elaborate scenarios of use. Humour is effectively used as a means to engage user audiences. Critical design practice employs satire as a particular form of humour. Satire is the art of diminishing a subject by making it ridiculous and evoking attitudes of amusement, contempt, scorn, or indignation towards it. In design's various critical practices, satire functions as constructive social criticism. This is done with the intent of shaming individuals, the discipline, and society into improvement. Satire has long been used as a device to offer critique, but it also provides a provocative lens by which to examine design's forms of critical practice.

Critical design practice delivers a satiric response to disciplinary, scientific, or social concerns. Literary satire, with its established theoretical foundation, can be used to show how satire functions in critical design practice. Satire often takes the form of the genre it spoofs. This is important as critical design practice functions as a commentary by subverting product design, while at the same time refusing to abandon design principles. A function of critical design practice, in line with the function of satire, is constructive social criticism. In achieving this, the designers use wit as an instrument to afford critical reflection. Design functioning in this way holds vices, abuses, and shortcomings found in orthodox product design, scientific developments, or sociocultural conditions up to ridicule.

An issue is criticized because it falls short of some standard that the designer, as critic, desires that it should reach. Inseparable from any definition of satire is its corrective purpose, expressed through a critical mode that ridicules or otherwise attacks those conditions needing reformation in the opinion of the satirist designer. There is no satire without this corrective purpose; therefore, critical design practice is only critical design practice if it has corrective purpose. Satirists induce the audience to protest and as a result, the language of the satirist is full of irony, paradox, antithesis, colloquialism, anti-climax, obscenity, violence, vividness, and exaggeration. Thus, satire attempts to affect some changes in the behaviour of the target as well as to encourage others not to behave in such a manner. Among the strategies are exaggeration, distortion, understatement, innuendo, simile, burlesque, metaphor, oxymoron, parable, and allegory.

There are two broad forms of satire named after the classic roman satirists who developed the styles. Horatian satire, named after Horace, is optimistic, less political, humorous, and identifies folly. While, Juvenalian satire, named after Juvenal, is the opposite of horatian with a focus on evil, political, and savage ridicule. These forms of satire are useful to consider in a theoretical analysis of critical design. Juvenalian satire works through narrative techniques of antithesis, obscenity, and violence, whereas horatian is much more playful and reflective, operating through exaggeration, burlesque, and metaphor. We will see in Chapter 5 how the form of satire employed in design work is a useful mechanism to differentiate between types of critical design practice.

These affective and communicative methods augment orthodox approaches to product and industrial design. They extend a conventional understanding of function and ultimately extend the agency of product design to become an instrument of inquiry, provocation, and change as much as an instrument to drive innovation, commercial, and technological interests.

Conclusion

This chapter presents a review of theoretical concepts, methods, and tactics in critical design practice. Design that functions to generate debate and engage user audiences in discussion on and around issues within contemporary design, culture, science, technology, and society is essential for the disciplinary development of product and industrial design. This application of the industrial designer's skill set offers a complementary perspective to that of the designer driven by fiscal and technologically centred concerns. Such a practice is used to deepen our understanding of industrial design. This role allows for exploration, reflection, and engagement. The focus here is not on the intrinsic materiality of the object but on the symbolic and existential function of objects and their systems of use. These characteristics are amplified through the integration of purposeful ambiguity and paradox used as mechanisms that are embedded in the design and definition of the work. Such mechanisms afford a dilemma of interpretation on the part of the user. Diverse publics are constructed around the object and it is in the interactions within this public assemblage where conversations are started, debate occurs, and the system that the design work exists in – either real or fictional – can be challenged and discussed. Therefore, utility in this practice resides in its ability to form publics and the interactions, conversations, thinking, and inquiry that are catalysed by the projects. Working in this way, critical design practice is being embraced by the sciences and in sociological discourses; critical design practice suggests a role for design processes as a way to develop cultural critiques of matters of concern ranging from the biosciences, bioengineering, biomedicine, environmental science, and much more because its socialization and positioning institutionally and intellectually push it towards public contexts. Design speculating in this way questions if these design practices are a better way to develop practical understandings for engineers, designers, and applied scientists of their roles in shaping social conditions and technological futures. In short, this is because facts and solutions end debates but evocative design opens up debates and is a powerful way to question hegemonic thinking. Rather than aiming for transparency, as in conventional practice, the approaches attempt to enhance the critical distance between the object and the human subject through the introduction of poetic techniques of aesthetic, fiction, defamiliarization, estrangement, designing ambiguity, and producing non-rational objects. Operating in this way, critical design focuses more intently on interpretive use where subjectivity and ambiguity are seen as a positive and constructive mechanism. The user participates in constructing meaning around the object and these constructions provide evidence for problem finding in disciplinary and societal discourse.

The examples discussed in the chapter and the theoretical positions introduced demonstrate an extended agency for product and industrial design where the discipline is moving to address concerns that perhaps are not typical to product and industrial design. However, while these communities embrace the practice, there is work to do to establish and develop a complete understanding of the value of critical design in a disciplinary context. The following chapter will begin to question the contribution of critical design to the product and industrial design discipline and profession.

4

CRITICISM, FUNCTION, AND DISCIPLINE

This chapter considers some barriers and misconceptions to critical design practice being seen as part of a disciplinary project. The first part of the chapter reviews the criticism of critical design to identify inadequacies in how the criticism is grounded. Analysis of critical design practice often comes from perspectives developed in art and visual culture discourses; however, analysing the practice from this perspective has limitations. Instead, the chapter argues how a more design-centric focus is needed. The second part of the chapter discusses 'function' – a concept often used to ground criticism of critical design practice but, again, one that has limitations. Function offers insufficient grounds for criticism and claims that critical design is *not* a form of product design because the objects do not 'function' in a utilitarian sense. The chapter explores the concept of function to show not only that an object's function has the potential to extend beyond utility, efficiency, and optimization, but also that even in the strictest modernist sense, function has always comprised characteristics that move into post-optimal realms – beyond efficient use, utility, and practical specifications. The chapter argues instead for an emphasis on the relational, dynamic characteristics of function that support seeing and discussing critical design practice in the same manner that other examples of orthodox product and industrial design are discussed. The discussion goes on to contextualize critical design practice in relation to a disciplinary core by considering the focus of critique, commentary, or inquiry directed through design work.

Design art

Criticality as a concept connected to the operations of design and culture has deep and debated roots. Such criticism is often steeped in the history of aesthetics, philosophy, and art history. However, criticality in industrial design, which is filtered through design theory and research, is still in its infancy even if related discussions, papers, and conferences have seen a clear increase in the past few years. As critical design practice has developed, looking to disciplines outside industrial design for theoretical insights has made sense. Where efforts in this direction have been undertaken, they focused in areas such as aesthetics and visual culture but because of critical design's proximity to conceptual art, an art-based critique of the practice emerged. This connection is evident in how commentators have characterized the practice as a form of 'design art' that according to Joe Scalan's definition 'could be defined loosely as any artwork that attempts to play with the place, function, and style of art by commingling it with architecture, furniture, and graphic design' (Coles 2002).

In a similar way, the design critic Hal Foster argues that in many examples of contemporary practice, design work is being consumed and traded as art, and so design and art are running together. From this perspective, where design is consumed in the gallery space and critical design objects are available for purchase by price on application, critical design becomes subject to art discourse.

Contextualizing critical design practice within this discourse, Aaron Betsky describes critical design as a hybrid between fine art and design (Betsky 2003, 14). Remy Ramakers describes critical design in terms that make it sound more like art than design, claiming that it strives 'to arrive at new aesthetic and conceptual potentials' (Ramakers 2002, 41) and Jamer Hunt writes that critical designers explore 'a messier emotional landscape of fear, pain, erotic attachment, and loneliness' (Hunt 2003, 41). Moreover, Hunt suggests that critical design operates outside functionalist frameworks because it develops a thesis that 'the inability of design to tap into this reservoir of emotional attachments impoverishes us' (Hunt 2003, 41).

Suggesting a hybrid form of practice, design commentator Rick Poynor writes that critical design blurs the boundary between design and fine art in the field of industrial design (Poynor 1999). He elaborates on an assertion by critic Alex Coles that when designers reflect on authorship, they invariably claim 'some kind of right to their own measure of self-expression' and in the manner claimed by artists, he claims that 'few have much to say about the role of design in society, or about anything else' (Coles 2005). Poynor has singled out the work of Dunne and Raby, as well as Hella Jongerius, as examples of designers who 'exceed their functional role', claiming that 'they challenge expectations of conventional form and the possibilities of product design' (Poynor 2005).

By embracing a concept of function beyond practical functionality, critical designers strive for an extended role for the designer. In their extended role, designers use their functional capacity as designers, still drawing on their training and practice as designers but re-orienting these skills from a focus on practical ends to a focus on design work that functions symbolically, culturally, existentially, and discursively. Practical and efficient use is not the purposive function. Functionality in this context is linked to stimulating debate, i.e. design for debate.

Design art and society

Critical design practice in many cases examines the social agency of design. Designers do so by looking at objects of design in their social contexts, by observing daily conditions and practices. They look at how design activity might inquire into social and technical concerns, pass comment on them, or bring publics together to address them. In such scenarios, the designers are acutely aware of industrial design's agency in both disciplinary and societal frames. Moreover, the sociological perspectives that increasingly inform so much of the practice are steeped in deep studies that pay enormous attention to the social and relational character of objects.

Given the relational character of industrial design, the relative newness of the turn towards an in-depth focus in these areas is surprising. However, in recent years, an increasingly energetic dialogue has emerged between design, social science, and scientific disciplines. Much of this dialogue has been aimed at enabling mutual understanding, identifying shared intellectual interests, and exploring common frames of reference.[1] Such conversations are nowhere more evident than in the work carried out at the Interaction Design Research Studio at Goldsmiths University. The studio outwardly embraces the dialogue between design and sociology through a number of collaborative critical and speculative design projects.

Recent design work and research has included the *Energy and Co-Designing Communities (ECDC)*. *ECDC* is a co-design project developed as a collaboration between the departments of sociology and design at Goldsmiths, University of London; it combines methods of co-design with speculative design challenging any separation between ethnographic research and speculation. In 2014, *ECDC* distributed the *Energy Babble* devices to thirty homes. *Energy Babble* is a domestic appliance that broadcasts comments and sounds sent from a network of Babbles. *Energy Babble* is familiar, playful, and ambiguous; it is designed to provoke debate within communities by exploring the imaginative and emotional dimension of energy use. Funded by the Research Councils UK (RCUK) Energy Programme, the project has a serious function through its exploration into how the United Kingdom can reduce its energy consumption by 80 per cent before 2050.

The initiatives led by Natalie Jeremijenko in the *Environmental Health Clinic* at New York University also focus attention on sociotechnical systems that object of use exist in. The clinic is set up much like the kind you would visit for an ear infection or sprained ankle, but its services are not of the medical sort. The project approaches health from an understanding of its dependence on external local environments, rather than on the internal biology and genetic predispositions of an individual. Visitors to the clinic – who Jeremijenko terms 'impatients' because they are individuals who do not want to wait for legislative change – must make

Figure 4.1 A and B Interaction Research Studio: Energy and Co-Designing Communities, Practitioners and researchers imagining energy communities. Production version of Energy Babble, 2014. Bill Gaver, Mike Michael, Tobie Kerridge, Liliana Ovale, Matthew Plummer-Fernandez, and Alex Wilkie, 2014.

an appointment to discuss their environmental concerns. At the end of the consultation, they leave with a prescription not for pharmaceuticals but for design interventions that they can do themselves. Such interventions might be anything from collecting data on the environmental quality of the local neighbourhood to creating a participatory public art project that increases community awareness of a particular concern.

This common area between the social sciences and critical design practice is generating much interest, where critical and speculative design work is being presented in social science forums. For example, the Speculation, Design, Public and Participatory Technoscience: Possibilities and Critical Perspectives forum, held at the 2010 conference of the European Association for the Study of Science and Technology, brought together designers and social scientists to discuss technological development and public debate through design.[2] In a similar respect, Anne Galloway is noted for organizing platforms and opportunities to discuss how grounded ethnographic and action research methods can be transformed into fictional and speculative designs, the purpose of which is to give people the kinds of experiences and tools that can lead to direct community action in the development and implementation of new technologies.[3] Moreover, Alison Clarke's *Design Anthropology* documents a collection of accounts that discuss the effects of critical design practice in sociological terms (Hunt 2011). In *Design Anthropology*, Hunt reconsiders his earlier thesis by which he aligned critical design with conceptual art; the problem with critical design now, he asserts, is that it remains close to an art practice, especially in its framing in the gallery space. Hunt questions what effect critical design can have on real-world design, which persists in operating in the name of opportunism.

Activity in this area undoubtedly illustrates that not all 'critical' designers aspire to be artists, and how the designs only 'work' if they are viewed as industrial design and the objects are seen to operate in a system of use beyond the gallery's white walls. When the designer's intention is that the work be seen as design, critique from the perspective of art can be distracting.

A problem with criticism grounded in art is that it feels like an attempt to fit critical design practice into a discourse in which product design aspires to be art, or at least places design on the same critical footing. Such discourse offers distinct examples of a narrow perception of design. For example, critics Hal Foster (2002) and Alex Coles (2007) adopt a theorem formulated by Baudrillard (1996) stating that design is limited to a sign exchange value and the symbolic dimension of objects. Furthermore as Moline (2006) argues, Poyner and Mermoz confuse the specificities of art and design practices in an unexamined adoption of relational aesthetics (Poynor 2005; Mermoz 2006). When work such as that carried out by Jeremijenko and the Interaction Design Research Studio, or for that matter any other example presented in this book, is discussed in these terms and when it is limited to sign exchange or described as social art, the danger is that the designer's focus underpinning the design work is overlooked.

For critical design practice to work as commentary or inquiry, its objects need to be viewed as industrial design. Looking at examples of critical design practice as pieces of art provokes a different discussion on and around the object rather than if it is analysed, criticized, and discussed as product design. The differences are exemplified in Dunne and Raby's 'Human Poo Energy Future, Poo Lunch Box' which probes social embargos towards individual energy production by collecting and processing human waste. The project provokes thought because of its proximity to everyday use. This strategy is outlined by Raby:

> While critical design might heavily borrow from [art] methods and approaches, it definitely is not art. We expect art to explore extremes, but critical design needs to be close to the everyday and the ordinary as that is where it derives its power to disturb and question assumptions. [...] It is only when read as design that critical designs can suggest that the everyday as we know it could be different – that things could change. (Raby 2008, 95)

The fact that design critics might have difficulties with critical design practice is understandable. A traditional design's success is often measured by how well it has worked within certain constraints, by the qualities of the idea, and by how well the idea has been executed using frameworks in which objects are 'fit for purpose' and of 'good form' – concepts that ultimately relate to the essentialist view of function and efficient use. Therefore, the challenge is to develop the means, the understanding, and the language to critique critical design. When engaging in discourses that are considered positioned outside of the product design discipline, as critical design projects often do, design critics need to tread carefully and rigorously. When a discipline shifts into new areas, analysing and critiquing become very difficult. In addition, designers can easily avoid confronting criticism by inferring that critics are misinterpreting a project's aims and purpose.

The danger of not questioning the critical design practice is evident in the contradictions that can be found in the writings and the curation of critical design work. Christina Cogdell (2009) describes this contradiction in her review of the exhibition *Design and the Elastic Mind.* In this exhibition, the design writer and curator Palo Antonelli uncritically positioned the adoption of living products as a sustainable organic design solution that would prevent the slaughter of cattle for leather and therefore would reduce the environmentally damaging cattle industry. Antonelli's account is one example of an idealized and somewhat optimistic appropriation of critical design practice.

Figure 4.2 Dunne and Raby, *Human Poo Energy Future: Lunch Box*, 2004. Photograph: Dunne and Raby.

The difficulty in critiquing and discussing critical design practice comes about because, unlike traditional designers, critical designers primarily focus on the communication of an idea, rather than the development of a product or service. Criticizing something that, like some art, defines its purpose as raising debate and communicating ideas is difficult. In effect, any criticism of the work can be perceived as debate and therefore can be seen as confirming its success. However, for critical design practice to work and contribute to a disciplinary foundation of product and industrial design, it must never be beyond criticism itself.

Function in critical design practice

Moline and Mazé argue that an overly reflexive practice, discussed in the same way that art practice is discussed, is counterproductive in developing a critical design practice that contributes to and expands the purview of industrial design as a discipline[4] (Moline 2006; Mazé 2007). Moline calls for a more design-centric analysis of critical design practice. She argues that certain perspectives – for example, relational aesthetics – polarize the designer because the designer as author is antithetical to the designer as service provider.

Similarly, Pullin suggests that '… there are other design approaches between these two extremes' and that 'a richer shared vocabulary of the different roles of design in this area would be valuable' (2010, 731). This position is shared by Moline, who questions the givens of functionalist debates in design and argues for an extended vocabulary for critical, conceptual, and experimental practice:

> Despite the growing research in design history and contemporary practice, design criticism lacks density. Much design criticism is generally limited to reductive pragmatic and simplistic understandings of functionalism that emphasize market popularity and technical innovation to the neglect of the wider ramifications of design decisions. (Moline 2008)

Moline's argument has two important implications. First, she issues a call for designers, commentators, design critics, and theorists to develop the vocabulary they use to discuss critical design practice in terms not solely dependent on arguments and knowledge from other fields of expertise. Second, Moline identifies how the criticism of critical design practice from the arts and visual culture is often grounded in a somewhat narrow conception of function. This narrow conception, limited to practical functionality based on optimization and efficiency, is arguably the most prominent barrier to seeing critical design practice as industrial design. Therefore, to develop critical design practice as part of a disciplinary project, an understanding of function limited to practicality, optimization, and efficiency needs to be readdressed.

Because of historic connotations, function associated with practicality in use appears to be an easy concept to use to dismiss the critical design practice as something other than product design. However, function is far from being a clearly defined term and is widely discussed in literature on design.[5] The popular understanding comes from Louis Sullivan's observation in 1896 that 'form ever follows function', which was subsequently popularized in the modernist dictum, 'form follows function'.

In common understanding, function relates to optimization and efficient performance. Lemoine (1988) describes design as being grounded in modernity, which is why from its beginnings the design of things and their function have been geared towards the principle of optimization (i.e. the idea of a positivistic interpreted controllability of the world). This interpretation of function commonly designates the object's practicality in use. This perspective is exemplified in user-centred design, which employs some measure of user participation to optimize design with regard to practical and efficient use. Historically, this focus for designers and the strong faith in modernist ideology has provoked criticism. For example, Lemoine writes:

> This particular debate, in which modernism and functionalism are conflated, has tended to divert attention from the aesthetic to the tactical; there is nothing inherently 'modern' about 'function' – design has always had a functional element. (Lemoine 1988, 23)

Dormer also questions the optimization of products with regard to their function:

> This is what differentiates the 1980s from 1890, 1909, and even 1949 – the ability of industrial design and manufacturers to deliver goods that cannot be bettered, however much money you possess .... Beyond a certain, relatively low price, the rich cannot buy a better camera, home computer, tea kettle, television, or video recorder than you and I. (Dormer 1990, 124)

Criticism of modernist functionalism can be traced back to an overemphasis on the physical and essentialist characteristics. However, what function is and considers, even in the modernist sense of the term, is questionable.

Ligo challenges the foundations of modernist functionalism in an analysis of how function was discussed by modernist architectural critics (Ligo 1984). He shows that function is not limited to practicality in use and classifies five very different types of function:

- Structural articulation, which refers to the object's material structure;
- Physical function, which refers to the utilitarian task of the object;
- Psychological function, which pertains to the user's emotional response to the object;

- Social function, which refers to the nature of the activity that the object provides with regard to the social dimension; and

- Cultural-existential function, which has more profound cultural and symbolic characteristics that include the existential being of the individual using the object.

In similar terms, archaeologist Michael Schiffer writes that an object can have three different sorts of function. The most commonly understood is 'techno-function', which is where the object is up to the job at hand (Schiffer 1992). This understanding is similar to Ligo's 'structural articulation' and 'physical function'. Less frequent are his 'ideo-functions' that draw from sets of abstract ideas that we share, like Ligo's 'psychological' and 'cultural-existential' function. The third function Schiffer identifies is 'socio-function' that has parallels to Ligo's 'social function' as it signals to others the sort of attitude that we hold. In addition, Schiffer notes that, just as often, the function depends on where the object is, who is using it, and when; thus, function comes about because of the system in which an object exists so that the object's function is defined by the context of use. Schiffer calls this the 'system function'. By definition, system functions cannot be designed into objects. The system function comes about only in the process of users' interaction with the object as they create the systems in which the object functions (Fisher and Shipton 2010).

Much work has been done in this area in material culture studies. For example, Daniel Miller argues that function is a dynamic concept and open to interpretation in different social contexts; he writes that 'even the physicality of a material object in one social context might be read differently in another social context and the systems of use that pertain' (Miller 1987, 109). Miller extends his argument to suggest how the labelling and classification of an object are used to indicate both its function and the relationship between the object and how it is used. He also describes how objects often function beyond these prescriptions, in different systems of use:

In no domain is it as difficult as it is in the matter of function and utility to distinguish the actual place of artefacts in human practices. In many societies the classification and labeling of objects appear to indicate a close relationship between artefact and particular function. What is problematic about this is the common assumption that is caused by and in turn indicates some relationship of efficiency between the object and its use. (Miller 1987, 116)

In keeping with this convention, Kristina Niedderer in her thesis, introducing the category of performative object, is critical of reading function from an object's form. She writes:

Although the material form is one mode through which function becomes apparent, function is not equal to the form nor is it fully visible in the form. An object's function becomes fully visible in its second mode, in use, which is pinpointed in the definition of function as 'the special kind of activity proper to anything' (OED 2009). The definition emphasizes function as an immaterial quality that is bound to the dynamic use of the object. (Niedderer 2004, 64)

Describing how functions emerge in use, Kroes (2010, 85) argues that technical functions are related to physical features, but just as often, they are subject to human intentions. This thinking is expressed in practice-oriented design that assumes the relationality of meaning and states that values and meaning emerge in practice and in relations between objects, skills, and temporalities that, in turn, define an object's use:

When technologies appear stable, when their design is fixed, their social significance and their relational role in practice [are] always on the move (Bijker, 1992). This suggests that moments of socio-technical closure [are] illusionary in that objects continue to evolve as they are integrated into always fluid environments of consumption, practice, and meaning. (Shove, Watson, and Ingram 2007, 8)

In such conceptions, function is relative and situational; it is a dynamic property – a matter of concern, rather than something factual and fixed. Latour illustrates how an object might function in this way:

It was as if there were really two very different ways of grasping an object: one through its intrinsic materiality, the other through its more aesthetic or 'symbolic' aspects. The functionalist technical perspective sees the objects as a matter of fact; an alternative is to see the object as a thing, a matter of concern that is encompassing of object and system. (Latour 2009, 2)

These arguments suggest that an object's function cannot simply be read from its form, from the way that it is labelled or classified, or even from its physical properties. Function is a dynamic, immaterial, and social property. An object's function depends on the practices that situate it in a system of use. Function is subject to the designer's intention; however, it is also always open to interpretation by the user.

The argument that function can be interpreted has important implications for any criticism of critical design practice based on function. Function might be understood as the plan of action that the object represents, where designer and user share their understanding about the intended purpose of the object. The function of an object can therefore be as a symbolic communicating concept, and a matter of understanding between the designer and user. Function might be understood as the perception of use, which emphasizes the appropriation of the object through the user according to their particular needs, involving what Mazé describes as '… processes of interpretation, incorporation, and appropriation into the user's lifeworld' (Mazé 2007, 2). Therefore, like Schiffer and Niedderer, Mazé indicates that function has its counterpart in use, which means that although function and use are normally assumed to converge in the contextual understanding of efficient functionality, they do not have to do so. Function itself is open to wilful appropriation within use, and subject to the intentions of the user. Thus, an object's function is physically constructed but at the same time is a social construction so that objects of use have a dual ontological nature, as Kroes details:

> An essential aspect of any technical object is its function; take away from a technical object its function and what is left is just some kind of physical object. It is by virtue of its practical function that an object is a technical object. The function of technical objects, however, cannot be isolated from the context of intentional action (use). The function of an object, in the sense of being a means to an end, is grounded within that context. When we associate intentional action with the social world (in opposition to causal action with the physical world), the function can be said to be a social construction. So a technical artifact is at the same time a physical construction as well as a social construction: It has a dual ontological nature. (Kroes 2010)

In critical design practice, function moves beyond physical and technical function, optimization, efficiency, and utility to operate in social, psychological, and cultural-existential ways. This function is advocated in the tactics detailed in Chapter 3, for example, in Hällnas and Redström's meaningful presence and aesthetics of use, in Dunne's, para-functionality and post-optimal design, and in Ball and Naylor's correspondences and context.[6]

Objects that are conceived through these constructs might not serve a practical function, or the object's form might not illustrate its function, but it has a function through the assertion of the designer, through the contexts engendered in the work, and more importantly, through the user's willingness to read the object as product design. Through these factors, the context of use in which a critical design object functions is established.

Chapter 3 showed that in the most abstract examples of critical design practice, the intentions of the designer and the object's use are contextualized by writing, photography, or film. These mechanisms are used to establish scenarios of use and the competencies required to understand the work as design. The design works through a form of rhetorical function and use. Such a proposition is not so far removed from some established and widely accepted perspectives. For example, Richard Buchanan compares design to rhetoric, suggesting that:

> The designer, instead of simply making an object or a thing, is actually creating a persuasive argument that comes to life whenever a user considers or uses a product as a means to some end. (Buchanan 1989, 95)

Rhetorical use is a type of imagined and fictional use. If function is considered as a socially constructed concept, or as a matter of concern rather than a fact, then rhetorical use and para-functionality are as legitimate as practical function and actual efficient use. Through rhetorical use, critical design practice leverages practical functionality to achieve the primary goal of delivering a deliberate message that is potent enough to spark contemplation, discussion, and debate by allowing users to imagine using the object in their everyday life.

In this context, Vilém Flusser notes that objects are not objective but are inter-subjective and rife with the values and intentions of the person who designed them. In using objects, we interact with things projected by other people. Such a proposition does not just reside in the philosophical perspectives of Flusser. Writing from a more technical perspective, Van de Poel and Kroes share this understanding:

> Those who argue in favor of some kind of moral agency consider technical artefacts to be inherently normative: technological artifacts are not taken to be simply inert, passive means to be used for realizing practical ends. In other words, technological artefacts are considered to be somehow 'value-laden' (or 'norm-laden'). These moral values and norms may be explicitly designed into these artefacts, or they may be acquired in (social) user practices. (Van de Poel and Kroes 2006)

Objects of use are therefore mediations between one person and another and are not just objects. Flusser asks whether designing objects can be formulated in this way:

> Can I give form to my projected designs in such a way that the communicative, the inter-subjective, the dialogic are more strongly emphasised than the objective, the substantial, and the problematic? (Flusser 1999, 59)

Essentially, critical designers answer affirmatively and proceed accordingly. Through rhetoric and the acknowledgement of the dual ontological character of objects, and through the social construction of function and use, systems of use are established. Within this system of use, where the user is willing to see objects of critical design practice as product design, critical design practice *is* product design. However, here the 'critical' designer faces the full challenge: affording rhetorical and imagined use and establishing the competencies required so that the user understands the work as design.

In today's design culture, a barrier is built on the doctrine of technical function grounded in efficiency and optimization. The challenge for the critical designer is to overcome these barriers. Meanwhile, the challenges for the theorist and critic are to acknowledge a broader concept of function and to see and discuss critical design in a more design-centric discourse in order to coherently place critical design practice in its disciplinary and professional context.

The paradox of critical design in commercial use

The critical social theorist Craig Calhoun suggests that critical reflection on the way things are, with their underlying, often hidden factors, enables exploration of other possibilities, and can allow an improvement in the way things are (Calhoun 1995). How these critical practices improve the way things are is not an easy subject. On the one hand, enabling, affording, and evoking critical reflection, discussion, debate, and speculation is typically considered an improvement in itself. On the other hand, to make critique meaningful, it must be directed at those who contribute to the culture that is being critiqued (Koskinen et al. 2011). This would necessitate a movement out of the gallery, and the perception of critical design as intellectual debates 'by designers for designers'. It would also shift the role of debate from an end to a means. I have discussed the instrumental use of critical design in design research and as an effective tool in contexts of science and technology, but there are a limited number of examples where critical design has been used instrumentally in a product design industry context.

It could be argued that the technology company Philips carries out activity in this area. Gardien's (2006) design-led horizon innovation model proposes a framework that Philips designers use to think about short-, medium-, and long-term futures. Horizon 1, horizon 2, and horizon 3 reflect short-, medium-, and long-term futures. Each horizon explores a different time space and therefore needs a different foresight in design approach and input. Horizon 3 is about radical innovation and transformation and creates a space where critical design might have commercial application in its ability to provoke debate and test societal expectations. Deliverables range from scenarios and narratives to the creation of experience prototypes. An example of this is Auger's *Smell+* project (discussed in Chapter 5). Intel and Microsoft have also initiated briefs with research centres and universities to carry out work that might not align with core business but are conceived with an interest to probe future social, political, and economic expectations and possibilities. In such activity, the commercial sector recognizes design's ability to visualize and make issues tangible through scenarios of use and object form. Walker (2010) describes how design carried out from within an academic context can contribute in commercial, mainstream contexts as it confronts contemporary issues and complex problems:

> We must find ways to renew the profession by developing agendas and propositions that envision what is desirable, meaningful, and sustainable; the responsibility to do so lies partly with those in the profession itself and partly with the academic institutions that educate and train its future participants. (2010, 97)

He argues that design in academia has the opportunity to focus on fundamental, conceptual design in ways that are often more difficult to justify in corporate culture:

> Design at universities has the capacity and freedom to critique current approaches, examine their insufficiencies, and explore new possibilities in ways that are removed from the day-to-day priorities of design consultancy and, in view of the urgent requirement for alternative, more benign ways forward, it has an obligation to do so. (2010, 98)

In this process, the reflective activity from fundamental research has the potential to feed into commercial design and applied research. Walker identifies how it is important to recognize:

> that the contribution of Speculative Design work within academia is not to develop potentially viable 'solutions' that can be tested or measured against some predetermined, pragmatic criteria. Rather, its purpose is to probe and challenge our assumptions and to explore other, imaginative avenues that appear to be worthwhile. (98)

The objective of this kind of work is to raise questions. An important point recognized by Walker is that critical design practice can be situated as a form of fundamental creativity-based research driven by envisioning new possibilities, and this differs in emphasis and purpose than reactive problem solving governing product and industrial design.

Modelling the field

Critical and speculative design might be said to operate as an intersecting field of research and practice – discipline and profession. Fallman (2008) visualizes this space in a model that not only refers to academic research, but also includes knowledge gained through practice-based and explorative avenues. Fallman's *Triangle of Interaction Design Research* can be used to plot the position of activity in between three extremes: design practice, design exploration, and design studies. The differences between these three types of practice are primarily in tradition and perspective, rather than the methods and tools being used. In Fallman's model, 'design practice' denotes activities that are similar to commercial design work, carried out in commercial consultancy but with a difference in that the researcher becomes engaged in a particular design practice with an appropriate research question in mind. The research question is developed and explored through a reflective first-hand experience, either of the tools or processes, or proactive manner, through an already established research agenda that seeks to change how a specific technique is used. 'Design studies' most closely resembles traditional academic research where the aim is to contribute to the intellectual tradition and body of knowledge. 'Design exploration' is similar to design practice but differs in one key point in that it aims to explore 'what if' questions through the process of designing, rather than by answering a particular research problem. Design exploration is a way to comment on a phenomenon by developing an artefact that embodies the statement or question that the researcher is attempting to critique. Fallman's 'design exploration' is synonymous with critical design practice:

> The typical client is the researcher's own research agenda. These projects are often self-initiated. Design in this area neither is typically driven by how well the product fits into an existing or expected future market, nor based on the observed needs of a group of users. Rather, design becomes a statement of what is possible, what would be desirable or ideal, or just to show alternatives and examples: design exploration is a way to comment on a phenomenon by bringing forth an artefact that often in itself, without overhead explanations, becomes a statement or a contribution to an ongoing societal discussion. (Fallman 2008, 7)

In another mapping exercise, *Design* Act (2009) highlights and discusses contemporary design and design research practices that engage with political and societal issues. It traces current and historic tendencies towards critical practice that engages ideologically and practically and provides a forum to discuss these with practitioners, educators, curators, critics, and others in the fields of design. Rather than posing a critique from the outside, *Design Act* explores design methods, aesthetics, and techniques that mount what Mazé notably describes as 'criticism from within' – that is, designers who engage with social and political ideas in and through action within their own practice. *Design Act* expands conceptions about what design is and catalogues examples that might look like pedagogy, policy, or art rather than conforming to the familiar objects and objectives of product design (Ericson and Mazé 2011).

Design Act documents projects that inquire into the social agency of design. Alongside examples of critical design practice, it includes examples of work that are described as Socially Responsible Design. Socially Responsible Design can be described as being critical of prevailing design orthodoxy because it is driven by social concerns over fiscal gain. From the emergence of Papanek's *Design for the Real World* (1984) through to feminist design, environmentally sensitive eco-design, and to the focus on sustainability, product designers have been increasingly active in creating solutions and addressing issues relating to social responsibility. First outlined by Papanek (1984), refined by Whitely (1993), and implemented by the likes of John Thackara and Hillary Cottam (UK Design Council Red; Participle), Socially Responsible Design is often structured around 'design thinking' and its ability to address wicked and complex problems.[7]

Socially Responsible Design contains many ideas about how to deliver problem solving through design practice or how to appropriately address and serve users – rather than consumers, in the name of society. Gamman and Thorpe (2011) outline the limitations of definitions of Socially Responsible Design and argue that social design does not facilitate design activity that makes social commentary through objects that seek to change the consumer system. Advancing the discourse in Socially Responsible Design, they have introduced Socially Responsive Design. Bülmann and Wiedmer (2008) write that critical design is a form of Socially Responsive Design, positioning critical design as a practice that acts as a synthesizer for change in societal concerns. In these accounts, the scholars attempt to theme design thought, methods, and concepts beyond commercially oriented practice and delineate the conceptual horizon against which designers operate critically.

Design at users

Sanders (2006) and Stappers and Sanders (2008) support positioning critical design practice against other forms of social design. They position critical design as a form of design-led research in the expert mindset. This suggests that critical design is considered a 'top down' practice where the user is seen as a reactive participant, rather than an active participant in a project. This useful distinction separates critical design from other forms of social design practice. In socially responsible design, there is increasing emphasis on user participation in the design process. Such collaborative practices move design from design for users to design with, and even design by users in co-design practices. These models of practice are illustrated by the design methods employed by the Helen Hamlyn

Research Centre at the RCA, Liz Sanders's *Make Tools* initiative and the move to open source product design, for example Open IDEO.[8]

The character of critical design practice can be aligned with Vilém Flusser's argument – reductio ad absurdum – that design is obstructive and the most responsible way to design is to be less objective, to design for matters of concern, and to communicate intersubjectivity (1999, 59). The matter of concern in critical design practice is creativity, inquiry, and statement, rather than technical or social innovation in service to actual needs and this illustrated through the various accounts outlined previously that position critical design practice as proposition and problem finding rather than problem solving in disciplinary and societal frames. Critical design practice is considered an authoritative form of practice. The designer performs as author and critic. This critical design practice can be described as 'design at' users, where a polemic commentary is directed at a user audience to address concerns that may not be overtly apparent, or perhaps may not yet exist, in order to engage and enlist that audience in debate.

Directing critique through design practice

Considering the discussion so far, it is appropriate at this point to outline how the designer as author directs their critique and situates critical design practice's position in a disciplinary context. The discussion outlined in this chapter and Chapter 3 asserts that critical design is a form of product design. It is not, however, considered an orthodox form of design. Traditional, orthodox, and mainstream design practices form a disciplinary core. With politically and socially engaged practices, the purview of product design is challenged and the discipline is extended into new territories.

Critical design practice operates on the periphery of a disciplinary core. Working as a boundary activity, the designers focus their commentary through the production of design work to focus in one of two directions: inwards towards disciplinary concerns or outwards towards broader social and technical concerns. The designer's critique or inquiry comes from within product design practice. It is focused either on the discipline i.e. focused 'within' or focusing outside normal disciplinary bounds i.e. focused 'without'. In this model, the practice is hybrid in its character, a blend of theory and practice, a method of design research and design practice. Product design functions as a form of discourse, as an exploratory tool, and an affective medium. Facing not only inwards towards disciplinary foundations, the designers' criticism, commentary, and inquiries reach out to implicate other domains involved in the social construction and consumption of design. This includes a range of concerns, ideas, and practices in use that are external to what might 'normally' considered product design.

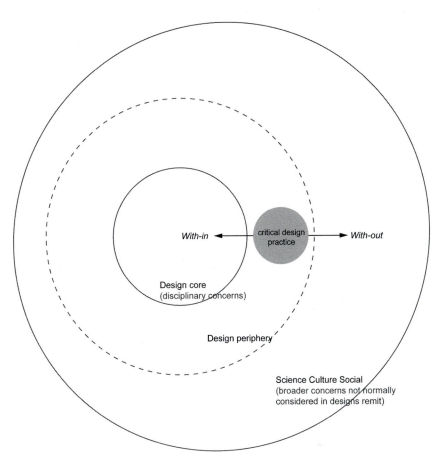

Figure 4.3 Operating context, focus of critique, commentary, or inquiry: critical design practice operates in a peripheral zone at the boundary of product design practice.

Conclusion

Although research into critical design practice is increasing, analysis of critical design has historically come from art and been grounded in theory more familiar to art and visual culture. This chapter has illustrated how analysis from the perspectives of art and visual culture is generally based on a somewhat limited concept of function. Such a perspective omits experimental, explorative, and discursive forms of design practice.

Challenging both the analysis and categorization of critical design as a form of art and a 'utilitarian' concept of function, the chapter has discussed the relational and dynamic characteristics of function as the means to ground key concepts in critical design practice. This discussion argues that even the most rigorously designed practical functions are interpreted. Function is a dynamic quality and open to wilful appropriation. Therefore, if both the designer and user are willing to see examples of critical design practice as design, then the work produced is design.

The discussion has outlined the need for a more design-centric focus on critical design. For critical design to work, the work needs to be seen as design and as it stands, the majority of theoretical engagement is grounded in art discourse. Discussing the objects of critical design practice as objects of design provokes a different discussion on and around the object than if it were discussed as art.

The chapter has outlined the need to engage a broader community in the discourse. Success in doing so might prevent the practice becoming overly self-reflective, subsumed as symbolism, and restricted to a cultural context. The discussions on the characteristics of function equip observers of critical design practice to overcome the barrier to seeing the practice as product design based on 'practical functionality', and rather to discuss the practice in design terms. For example, such discussion moves the discourse beyond aesthetic questions that might echo in the art gallery to questions about an object's use, the practices that situate it, behaviours that might emerge from the object's use, and the publics that form around the work. Thus, the chapter argues for a richer vocabulary in critical design, one that moves beyond the critical/affirmative dichotomy and for an analysis of the field that does not rely on other disciplines. The review of research into critical design practice worked to demonstrate the disciplinary positioning of critical design practice and its relationship to other exploratory practices, how it interfaces with industry as a form of fundamental research, and how it is positioned as operating at the periphery of the product and industrial design discipline challenging the disciplinary boundary. The following chapter explores a range of examples that demonstrate how critical design practice operates, directs critique, functions to generate debate, and acts as an effective agent in disciplinary and broader contexts.

5
PRACTICE

Since 2006, I have been researching critical design in a project that questions the disciplinary contribution of the practice. This project has involved an extensive review of the field as it has developed and gathered interest from within the design research community and design profession. My position, as it is presented in this chapter, has been informed by engaging with critical designers who have worked to define and popularize the practice and, moreover, by engaging with work that challenges and problematizes the practice. So far, I have discussed critical design's historic context and theoretical concepts that inform the tactics employed in addition to the disciplinary positioning of the critical practice. A number of examples have been used to illustrate the historic lineage and theoretical approach. In this chapter, I turn to focus on examples through the presentation of a taxonomy of practice that categorizes three distinct approaches to critical practice in product and industrial design. All may be fitted under the overarching rubric 'critical practice' of design, but these may further be differentiated and presented as associative design, speculative design, and critical design. This categorization of practice is useful because it expands the concept of critical design beyond its association with a relatively small community of practice and contributes to a broader discourse of critical practice within the product and industrial design discipline.

I define the first category of critical practice as associative design. This practice draws on mechanisms of subversion and experimentation that were first developed in conceptual art, but that were taken up by designers and employed to critique governing mentalities in industrial design. Associative design has its roots in political forms of Italian critical design and anti-design. The critique in this category focuses on disciplinary concerns. The second category of critical design practice is defined as speculative design. This term is increasing in popularity and its use in defining and describing projects. We have seen in previous chapters how this category of practice focuses on science and technology and advances product design to comment on emerging science and technology by drawing on socioscientific research and theories. The final category of practice I will introduce is critical design. Critical design as an approach critiques current social, cultural, technical, and economic controversies and hegemony through designing critical artefacts. It challenges conventional approaches in designing human object interactions. If we were to consider the historic lineage and trajectory of these practices, associative design came first, then critical design, and most recently speculative design. These three approaches in critical practice function as a form of satiric design. In each case, the designers use satire in their work to establish critique and engage user audiences in debate on and around the work.

The characteristics of satire and the range of techniques used to offer a satiric response through design are a useful means to differentiate between these three categories of critical practice. Mechanisms of satire, object rationality, and narrative are identified as instrumental in critical design practice. How these mechanisms are applied vary in associative, speculative, and critical design. The taxonomy introduced aims to explore important nuances in the field, noting differences between forms of critical practice while also problematizing the colloquial understanding of critical design. It functions as an analytical tool with which to frame practice, but also to understand the approaches at play in the various forms of critical practice.

The discussion throughout the chapter ultimately shows how contemporary critical design practice is a rich and diverse activity and that critical designers engage with a range of diverse themes. The chapter introduces each category of practice before describing projects placed in each of the three categories. Each project description considers what is being criticized and why. The examples discussed identify precise points inherent to the critical attitude in industrial design.

Associative design

Associative design primarily focuses on disciplinary content. The work in this category takes a critical view of the design discipline by offering a criticism from within design practice, which focuses on disciplinary concerns. The aim of this approach is to present the means for both designers and users to rethink dominant traditions and values in designed objects and their environment – where the design object is subjected to critical processes of refutation. Design methods, design's relationship to manufacture, materials, sustainability, habits in consumption, and questions of sustainability are typically taken as the object of inquiry, exploration, and critique.

With an embedded narrative, objects of associative design act as a critical medium, playfully reflecting on cultural meaning and visualizing issues pertinent to design practice today. It is a laconic form of design practice; it leans towards artistic speculation rather than design for production. I describe it as laconic, because unlike critical and speculative design it uses few words;

objects of associative design speak for themselves and do not need the contextualizing narrative so essential in examples of critical and speculative design.

Associative design works by subverting expectations of, and interactions with, ordinary, everyday product design. It functions through the subversion of conventional association and understanding of objects, and the subversion of the object or its context of use. Its objects are often reliant on a user's familiarity with form, object typology, and design language. It is in the subversion of this familiar understanding that the critical move is established, and the user is prompted to question the object. It challenges ideas, orthodox traditions, and the users themselves by playfully subverting this familiarity and associations, hence, 'associative'. It challenges embedded assumptions of products, making use of conventional disciplinary frames to assert and subvert norms. Associative design ultimately makes familiar objects strange.

The critical narrative is embedded into the object form and typically familiar archetypes. The practice is therefore dominated by furniture design with chairs, tables, and examples of lighting characterizing associative design. While appearing slightly strange, these archetypes are 'more-rational' in form and function than examples of speculative and critical design.

In associative design, designers employ a straightforward attitude to materials, an inventive approach to fabrication processes and methods, and typically a resistance to product styling. Associative design works through ambiguity of context where methods of 'cut up', 'context transfer', and 'hybridity' – as detailed in Chapter 2 – are used to intervene in concepts and behaviours engaged in use to establish ambiguity of context. Latent humour and dry wit characterize the objects. Associative design operates through Horatian satire, where methods of burlesque and parody, achieved through distortion, exaggeration, and understatement, are employed to engage the user and establish the critical move.

Examples of associative design include *Foam Matters: The Model World Maquette* (2007) by Dutch designer Jurgen Bey. In this example, Bey analyses the qualities, as well as cultural and emotional meanings, of the things in the built environment to provoke discussion about the value of the contemporary production processes. Bey places a strong emphasis on the design process in the majority of his product design. In this project, he positions the model – normally conceived as a means rather than an end in product design – as being particularly important as a tool for pursuing ideas beyond the constraints imposed by industrial production. Through the modelling process, and using materials such as cardboard and the ubiquitous styrofoam (blue foam) familiar to any student or industrial design professional, he refers to something that does not yet exist but takes an ideological view of examples of situations and uses of design that should exist more widely. The work operates as a parody;

the styrofoam material choice in the design of the desk and chair is impractical when proposed as a finished object, contradicting its function as furniture. This requires the user to look harder and closer at the object and the representation of a designed world that Bey stages within the model. The work ultimately presents a simulacrum of an unachievable reality and is inherently contradictory. It's in this contradiction that the question is asked: what would need to change in our approaches to design and production in order to reduce the contradiction and to realize the world as Bey proposes?

Spanish designer Marti Guixé has described himself as an ex-designer who expresses protest against the increasing dominance of economic laws in the design market. In critiquing this convention, Guixé sets up laws that he wishes the market to submit to before breaking those laws himself. The expression is intended to send a message that says that he can go beyond the boundaries traditionally assigned to the design discipline but without leaving the profession behind. His critique of product obsolescence and pursuit of the new is overtly demonstrated in *Statement Chairs* (2004). The chair, imbued with political slogans in Guixé's trademark typography, states its point and questions consumption and obsolescence. Through mechanisms of distortion, Guixé changes the perspective of a condition by emphasizing the ubiquitous garden chair and isolating its perceived disposable characteristics and lack of value. The object provokes the users to question their relationship to this object and by extension the whole category of throwaway products.

Italian designer Martino Gamper's associative design work can be characterized by spontaneity and the collapse of the processes of design and making. In *100 chairs in 100 days* (2007), Gamper uses satiric mechanisms of burlesque, afforded through methods of 'cut up' and 'hybridity', to recombine elements of existing chairs into a series of unique seats. Gamper focuses on creating situations that include materials, techniques, individuals, and spaces, and which favour meetings and discussion. His interest in the psychosocial aspects of furniture is translated in the use of unwanted objects to create a disparate family of objects. Adopting a situationist-like strategy – a set of rules or a programmes to operate by – 100 chairs in 100 days involved systematically collecting discarded chairs over two years, and then spending 100 days reconfiguring the design of each one in an attempt to transform its character and function. Gamper's intention was to investigate the potential for creating useful new designs by blending stylistic or structural elements of existing chair types. The project suggests a new way to stimulate design thinking and provokes debate about a number of issues, including value and different types of functionality. It draws attention to obsolescence, clutter, and the vernacular, and how these concerns are managed in practice.

Gamper's approach is echoed in the work of Brazilian designer Paulo Goldstein's *Repair is Beautiful* (2012). In *Repair is Beautiful*, through processes

Figure 5.1 *Statement Chairs*, experimental work of Marti Guixé. Lima Skip Furniture, 2004, Milan.

of distortion, Goldstein obsessively repairs and embellishes found objects exaggerating their status. This process of making is used to give back a feeling of personal control – projecting frustration upon broken objects that can be repaired through design and craftsmanship. The final outcome is a collection of intriguingly repaired objects imbued with meaning and functionality. The once rejected objects are given a new status. Through the project, Goldstein critiques cultures of obsolescence and embraces scarcity to provide material to design with.

Figure 5.2 Paulo Goldstein. Repaired Director Chair. Repair Is Beautiful, 2012. © Paulo Goldstein. *Repair Is Beautiful*, 2012.

In another example of associative design, the German furniture and lighting designer Julia Lohmann examines user relationships with the natural world. In *Cow Benches: A Leather Bench or Bovine Memento Mori* (2005), Lohmann makes comment on consumer relationships with animals and the production of them to meet consumer needs. Through burlesque and exaggeration the benches, in their familiar but contorted form, remind the user where materials come from. The Cow Bench explores the threshold between animals and materials by presenting a highly finished leather bench in a form that is not far removed from the raw material from which it is made. The work critically questions how consumers have become alienated from modes of production and the reality of where our products come from, encouraging us to consider this relationship through uncanny form.

British designers Ralph Ball and Maxine Naylor use methods of burlesque in associative design. In *Chair Anatomy* (2008), waste furniture is cut up, distorted, and reassembled to exaggerate its structure, assembly, and function. Their *24 Star Generic Office Chair* (2003) satirizes the common desk chair. Although ubiquitous today, similar chair designs were initially criticized for only having three legs on its base. Shortly after its production, the design was modified to make it more stable. Later secretarial chairs were required to have five legs on their base. Ball and Naylor preserve these criticisms in a chair form, adding a five-legged base to the original four. Thus, in the design, they articulate the chairs' history while making criticism on a culture of obsolescence. This is an extreme example of form following function. In the horatian approach, they employ mechanisms of reductio ad absurdum. The essential quality of burlesque is the discrepancy between subject matter and style. That is, a style ordinarily dignified may be used for nonsensical matter, or a style very nonsensical may be used to ridicule a weighty subject. The designers challenge the modernist dictums that have governed product and industrial design for so long.

Challenging the product design profession's role in fuelling cultures of production and mass consumption is a salient theme in associative design practice. A recent and notable example in this category is British designer Thomas Thwaites's *Toaster Project* (2009) through which Thwaites explores how we are alienated from the manufacture of domestic products in consumer society. In the project, Thwaites set about making a toaster from raw materials. His design process involved everything from mining the materials through to the design, production, and assembly of the toaster's components. The project questioned the contrast in scale between the products we use and the industry that produces them. The laboriousness of producing the most basic material from the ground up exposes the fallacy in a return to some romantic ideal of a pre-industrialized time. Thwaites suggests that at a moment in time when the effects of industry are no longer trivial in relation to the wider environment, the throwaway toasters of today seem unreasonable. Through exaggeration and overstatement, he delivers a toaster and questions if the provenance and the fate of the things we buy are too important to ignore.

While the typology is very familiar, in this example, the process and the documentation of producing the toaster were equally as important. The *Toaster Project* demonstrates an element of performativity that exists in examples of associative design. This performative approach to designing familiar objects that deliver poignant messages is demonstrated in the collaboration between the

Figure 5.3 Ralph Ball and Maxine Naylor, *24 Star*, Archaeology of the Invisible 2005. © Ralph Ball and Maxine Naylor, *24 Star*, 2005. Photographer: David Spero.

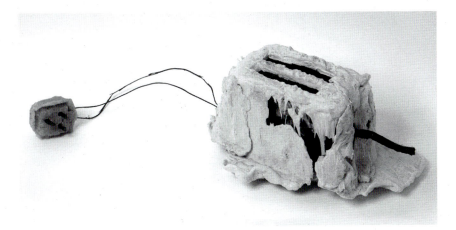

Figure 5.4 Thomas Thwaites. *The Toaster Project*, 2010. Photographer: Daniel Alexander.

designer maker Kieren Jones and Studio Swine (Alexander Groves and Azusa Murakami) in their *Sea Chair Project* (2010). This design work asks the question: how can we solve the problem of accumulating plastic in our oceans? A pool of plastic waste floats in the Pacific Ocean that is already double the area of the United States. This plastic waste does not sink and it takes thousands of years to degrade. Plastic fragments include a large amount of nurdles – plastic pellets about 2 mm in diameter that are the virgin raw material for injection moulding. These nurdles can be found littered on almost every shoreline in the world, and the United Nations estimates that there are 13,000 nurdles floating in every square mile of the ocean. In working with this problem, the design team aimed to turn a retired fishing trawler into a plastic chair factory, fishing the plastic from the polluted seas and beaches around the South West coast of the UK.

The designers proposed European Union plans to pay fisherman for catching plastic and proposed advances in the development of nets for collecting plastics with minimal damage to marine wildlife. Driven by a social and regenerative agenda, a floating factory ship that recycles this marine waste into sea chairs would support fishing communities and make use of their rich and diverse skillsets. Integral to this plan is the *Nurdler*, a hand-powered water pump that sorts microplastic from larger and denser materials and collects washed up plastic from the shore to collect material to produce the *Sea Chair*. The designers' engagement and the production of the chair are used to critique and generate debate about this environmental pollution.

Welsh designer Kieren Jones's critical practice focuses on systems of production emphasizing novel approaches to closed-loop sustainable production that counter hegemonies and stimulate debate around the impact of mass production. His work *Personal Micro-Farm: The Chicken Project, Backyard Factory* (2009) consists of three units: the first houses chickens,

Figure 5.5 Chicken Factory/© Kieren Jones 2009.

another prepares its skin for turning it into leather that Jones uses to style a flight jacket – bare in mind chickens are flightless – and a third unit bakes its ground-up bones into fine china to produce an egg cup – there is essentially enough chicken bone in one chicken to produce one average size egg cup.

Jones's proposal suggests a model of community-based self-sufficiency that becomes the status quo. Through the production of humble objects, though archaic material processing techniques, Jones – like Thwaites and Lohmann – raises questions about alienation and sufficiency in a culture of material consumption. Jones masterfully employs the understatement as a satirical tactic in his design work, the straightforward logic applied in the function of the objects proposed in the *Personal Micro-Farm* and *Sea Chair* are juxtaposed by the enormity of the problems they critique. The focus on a specific narrative and typology makes engaging with the complex discourses of environmental sustainability more manageable. The familiar objects are iconic of a targeted critique of the capitalist model of production and consumption and its effect.

Speculative design

Situated between emerging scientific and technological themes and material culture, speculative design operates in an ambivalent space; it typically focuses on the domestication of up-and-coming ideas in the sciences and applied technology. It is concerned with the projection of sociotechnical trends, developing scenarios of product roles in new use contexts. It is linked to futures, scenario building, and technoscientific research. It is characterized by this inquiry into advancing science and technology. It aims to broaden the contexts and applications of work carried out in laboratories and show them in everyday contexts. Rather than presenting utopic or dystopian visions, speculative designs pose challenging statements that attempt to explore ethical and societal implications of new science and the role product and industrial design plays in delivering this new science. The aim is to make scientific theories and the cultural implications of science perceptible in different ways. The practice questions and reflects on the implications of design decisions made today, and how they may proceed into the future. Speculative design encourages the user to reconsider how the present is futuring, that is, how innovative science and technology that might have seemed a long way off is actually being introduced to everyday material culture. When we actively consider the introduction and effect of this science and technology, we might potentiality have the chance to reconfigure the future. It considers biotechnology, nanotechnology, synthetic biology, robotics, and artificial intelligence as falling within design's remits.

Speculative designers advocate a democratic and open discussion into how science and technology is developed and directed. It serves as an alternative to existing strategies by channelling research findings through material objects. Rather than being represented as situated consumer products intended for mass production, these forms live in exhibition and public environments. What speculative design can do, with respect to this issue of public awareness and action, is frame situations or problems, inform user audiences about details of which they may not be aware, and even personalize and make intentionally mundane the experience of users facing life-changing events and challenges. But, speculative design avoids focusing on magic technologies and narrative resolution in order to offer critical analysis of implications and developing useful pathways to action.

Typically, speculative critical designers work with scientific practices, materials, concepts, and scientists themselves. Scientific instruments or materials, for example, petri dishes, tissue culture, MRI, and thermal imaging become part of the work. The results generated in scientific practice are taken up in the design work, and in some examples, the process of doing science itself has figured as the design process.

Because it is concerned with emerging science and technologies, the object propositions are often unfamiliar and therefore speculative design works through an ambiguity of information. The speculative design object is dependent on the construction of external narratives and scenarios of use. This is typified through methods of technocratic visualization, where the objects and the science they address are often depicted through film, image, and other documenting material that contextualizes the technology in use. Speculative designs are typically positioned in familiar, everyday domestic contexts that exaggerate the technology and encourage reflection on the information inherent in the work. This approach, taken to designing futures, is described as 'future mundane'. The futures rendered in speculative design are not slick shiny visions of the future; the scenarios are presented with contemporary hooks. Speculative designers situate speculative objects in a world of objects and environments that exist today. This strategy is grounded in an understanding that as we progress into a future, the material culture that exists today will not disappear; objects are collected and new innovations will sit alongside objects from time gone by. Scenarios of speculative design recognize this; the science and technology of a near future will be domesticated and presented alongside objects and environments that resonate with contemporary everyday life and material culture. These strategies embrace technology accretion: the drawer full of cables, the old interaction behaviours, the familiar hardware with its cracked screens, and scuffed housing. Rather than avoid this complexity in speculative design scenarios, we see emergent science and technology sit side by side with older artefacts, established practices of use, and behaviours. In some cases, this technique can be used to show potential disconnects and test sociocultural embargos that exist and might even inhibit the science and technology in question becoming real and progressing in the way the speculative designer proposes. This strategy of the future mundane allows the speculative designer to depict a more tangible future or compelling alternative present.

In constructing such scenarios and narratives of use, the speculative designer employs satiric mechanisms of understatement, distortion, and most importantly allegory. The 'mundane futures' or 'alternative presents', that is, the vision of how world might be that typify speculative design – and the science and technology in question – are often presented with very quotidian characteristics, but the science or technology is distorted to change the perspective of a condition or event by isolation (separation from its ordinary surroundings), or by stressing some aspects and de-emphasizing others. Through allegory, the critical message is more likely to be remembered in the speculation because of the vehicle of the story and its use of physical realities, that is, the objects, users, and interactions that are depicted to represent the concepts presented.

In developing their critical practice to focus more intensely on socioscientific futures, Dunne and Raby operate as speculative designers. In a number of projects, they question developments in technologies such as biotechnology and the opportunities such advancements might offer the product designer. A useful example to illustrate this approach, utilizing allegory, distortion, and the future mundane, is Dunne and Raby's 2010 work *Between Reality and the Impossible: Foragers*. This project works through techniques of distortion. By taking scientific activity out of the lab and into the fields, it anticipates a world dominated by overpopulation. Their *Foraging* project works through satiric techniques of distortion by taking scientific activity out of the lab as a means to address overpopulation through bottom-up, guerrilla tactics. Their allegory states that according to the United Nations, we need to produce 70 per cent more food in the next forty years; however, we continue to overpopulate the planet, use up resources, and ignore warning signs. Proposing a solution, they look at evolutionary processes, molecular technologies, and how we can take control of this situation. In essence, people will need to use available knowledge to build their own solutions and embrace the power to modify us. *Foragers* is essentially about the contrast between bottom-up and top-down responses to a massive problem and the role played by technical and scientific knowledge. It builds on existing cultures currently working on the edges of society who may initially appear extreme – guerrilla gardeners and garage biologists, for example. However, by adapting and expanding these strategies, they become models to speculate.[1] Other examples of Dunne and Raby's speculative design include *Consuming Monsters: Big, Perfect, Infectious* (2005) that examines a role for design in the debate about our biotechnological futures. In their *Bioland* project (2002–03), they also address the social and ethical implications of biotechnology through the presentation of an existential shopping centre with departments such as birth, death, and marriage in a genetically modified world. *Evidence Dolls* (2005) are used to provoke discussion amongst young women about the impact of genetic technology and how it affects their choice of lovers. The customizable plastic doll allows the users to visually describe their partner. A drawer allows the user to store a DNA sample in order to evaluate the genetic potential of lovers.

Italian designer Elio Caccavale's *MyBio* project investigates the moral, social, cultural, and personal responses to trans-human bioscience. Caccavale applies design in collaboration with bioethicists to explore issues surrounding reproductive technologies and family forms. He builds on an analysis of SciArt practices to develop a role for product design that fosters interdisciplinary dialogue between designers and scientists. Caccavale's methods are integrated with those of bioethicists with a view to use design proposals and assisted conception and surrogacy as case studies to make issues that surround life sciences more tangible for wider audiences. His design aims to provoke discussion about genetically modified human/animal hybrids in actual and near-future biotechnology. Collaborating with bioethicists Prof Richard Ashcroft (Imperial College London) and Prof Michael Reiss (Institute of Education, University College London), the project explores the relationship between children's learning of the categories of animals and humans and the extent to which such categories can be considered merely contingent and revisable in the light of technological change and advances in genetic engineering and synthetic biology.

Tobie Kerridge and Nikki Scott's *Biojewellery* presents the use of cultured bone tissue from two people as material for wedding rings. They collaborated with bioengineer Ian Thompson (King's College London) and science actually became part of the design process. The project was based on the premise that bone tissue cultivated outside a patient's body is used in reconstructive surgery to repair damage caused by injury or disease. As the science behind this process develops, it begins to spark curiosity, desire, and speculation about alternative uses of this technology and material. *Biojewellery* explored one alternative and used the techniques of bone tissue culturing to provide two couples with rings symbolizing their relationship. Their speculative design sought to provoke debate about the relationship between scientific progress and the public's imagination.

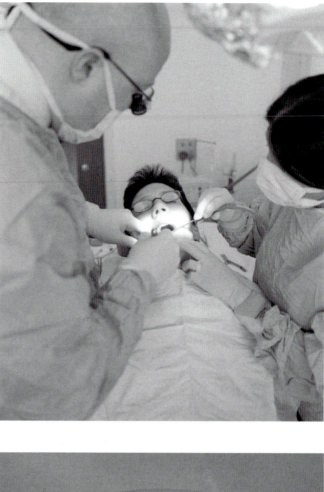

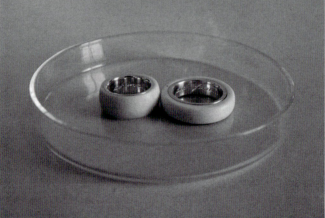

Figure 5.6 A and B Tobie Kerridge, Nikki Scott, and Ian Thompson, 2003, *Biojewellery*. Wisdom tooth extraction and models of Trish and Lynsey's rings, 2005–06. Photographer: Michael Venning.

Auger-Loizeau and Alex Zivanovic's *Carnivorous Domestic Entertainment Robots* (2009) propose an alternative perspective on domestic robots. The project explores the function that may afford the coexistence of humans and robots in the home. They resist a stereotypical form normally associated with robots and look more like household accessories. The robots utilize a microbial fuel cell as an energy source, a reference to the strategies of predatory insects, reptiles, and plants. In their allegoric narrative, Auger and Loizeau propose that the user might sit around the objects waiting for the moment when the prey is captured and slowly transformed into moving energy bars on the graphic display built into the objects, thus providing a dark form of entertainment. The project works through a form of distortion, a satiric technique that separates the object and technology from its ordinary surroundings, emphasizing some applications while playing down others. The technology is overdetermined for the function of the objects.

In another example of speculative practice and the domestication of scientific research, Auger's commission by Philips, *Smell+*, explores the human experiential potential of the sense of smell, applying contemporary scientific research in a range of domestic and social contexts. In one example, Auger speculates with objects that utilize dog's ability to detect cancer through the sense of smell so that the animal is used medically as a diagnostic tool.

Focusing on synthetic biology, Alexandra Daisy Ginsberg uses design to explore the implications of emerging and unfamiliar technologies. In *Growth Assembly*, she proposes that synthetic biology might enable the user to harness our natural environment for the production of products. Coded into the DNA of a plant, product parts grow within the supporting system of the plant's structure. When fully developed, they are stripped from their shells and are ready for assembly. In the proposed design, using biology for the production of consumer goods has reversed the idea of industrial standards, introducing diversity and softness into a realm that once was dominated by heavy manufacturing. The product components grown in *Growth Assembly* are proposed to come together to form a Herbicide Sprayer – a device to use in the culturing of more products.

Sputniko! (Hiromi Ozaki) is a Japanese designer who explores technology's impact on everyday life to imagine and speculate on alternative futures. Sputniko! invents devices and creates songs and music videos that include the devices in their diegesis. Although they serve as theatrical props, the devices are fully realized prototypes built in collaboration with scientists. Her work focuses on the social, cultural, and ethical implications of new technologies, often through the lens of feminism and gender issues. For example, Sputniko!'s *Menstruation Machine* is a device that allows a man to experience menstruation. It challenges repressed cultures in relation to gender and sexuality and instead of just making this object and then putting it in a museum, Sputniko!'s introduces it into Japanese pop culture by making it into a music video.

The context-specific domestication of technologies on the horizon is essential to engage users in debate. An effective example of this contextualization can be seen in the work of French designer Anne Couvert-Castéra and the speculative project *Hindu Tales – Souvenirs of a Future* (2015). The project questions the interactions of spirituality and technology. It focuses on Hindu devotees and imagines how they might use new technologies in their religious practice. Testimonies gathered from Hindus identified key questions about the Hindu identity and Hinduism's capacity to embrace the sociotechnical evolution of society. Through three allegories of a potential future for the Hindu community in a technological age, 'The Cab Altar', 'The Love Guru', and 'Connected Festivals', Couvert-Castéra depicts a scene from the everyday life of a person from the Hindu diaspora. She developed design responses using the Internet of Things, AI algorithmics, and digital manufacture to overcome the remoteness from 'Mother India', bringing to Hindus around the world a new way to live their spirituality and affording the sense of a global Hindu community.

In this scenario, the Patel family is celebrating the festival of 'Ganesh Chaturthi'. The festival involves installing clay images of Ganesh that are worshipped for ten days. The peak of the festival takes place on Mumbai's shores. The Patel family takes part in the festival remotely, thanks to their 'smart-shrine'. The family prays to their shrine, which hosts a 3D printer. As the family

Figure 5.7 Souvenirs of a Future: Connected Festivals/© Anne Couvert-Castéra. Hindu Tales 2015.

prays, the deity takes shape in front of their eyes. The smart shrine is printing a Ganesh idol with Ganges's mud as the family prays. In the meantime, the 'spiritual energy' of their prayer is transmitted to Mumbai where during the ten days of the festival, a large deity is 'printed' on Mumbai's shores. Through this project, Couvert-Castéra ultimately questions how design and technological development might interface with a tolerant and assimilative religious practice.

Dynamic Genetics vs. Mann by Superflux, part of the EU-funded research project blueprint's *For the Unknown* (2015), presents an example of speculative design working as a design fiction and the use of vignette to establish the allegory. *Dynamic Genetics vs. Mann* presents a landmark case in the fight against the theft of genetic medicines and the threat it poses to their continued development. The studio develops a story in the form of an evidence file that represents the body of evidence used in the prosecution of Arnold Mann, who is accused of receiving illegal, unlicensed copies of gene therapies owned by Dynamic Genetics. From tissue biopsy samples to an improvised CO_2 incubator used in the manufacture of counterfeit genetic therapies, *Dynamic Genetics vs. Mann* presents a body of evidence from a fictional court case. Unfolding as a rich narrative, the project explores a world where designed and patented genetic material enters the human body through illicit means. The work draws attention to the choice of scientific and technological progress, which is ultimately a political one. History has shown that political and economic forces exert as great an influence on the development and application of technology as the aspirations of scientists and engineers. Employing allegory to develop the satire and a critique of political and economic drivers that influence these technological trajectories, *Dynamic Genetics vs. Mann* explores synthetic biology, extrapolating from current social, economic, and political trends so as to locate the technology within a broader cultural landscape. This project presents a world in which synthetic biology and gene therapy have moved from the lab to the marketplace and questions the implications of this shift: what new legal and economic models might emerge under these conditions? How will intellectual property be applied and policed when designed genetic material makes its way into people's bodies and their lives? And who are the winners and losers in such a world?

Critical design

If speculative design focuses on science and the potential applications and implications of emerging technology, then critical design focuses on present social, cultural, and ethical implications of design objects and practice. It is grounded in critical social theory. Its designers scan the cultural horizon today, offering a critique of what already exists. At its core are para-functionality and the aesthetics of use. Through mechanisms of defamiliarization and estrangement, designers extend the critical distance between the object and the user; in so doing, they make striking comment on current sociotechnical, economic, political, cultural, and psychological concerns and find new forms of expression for complex issues. The critical approach is characterized by the articulation of the designer's viewpoint. Critical design shares traits with design activism and culture jamming.

In critical design, it is vital for the user to experience a dilemma and to carry something of a burden of interpretation. The intention is to engage audiences' imagination and intellect in order for the designer to convey the message. Examples of critical design often depict fictive scenarios but are at times also used to directly intervene in areas of oppression and inequality used as a disruptive mechanism applied to challenge hegemony.

Although they often employ familiar shapes, colours, and forms, such designs suspend the user uncomfortably between reality and fiction. They seem real but there is something not quite right; barriers are introduced or exaggerated in a way that is defamiliarizing. These mechanisms prompt the question: what would need to change in our reality to enable these products to exist in a normal model of consumption? It is in this tension between reality and what is prohibited that debate is encouraged. The aim is to expose assumptions, provoking action, and stirring debate.

Critical design works through what Gaver, Beaver, and Benford (2003) outline as relational ambiguity. The critical move is developed through a synthesis of the object and the media that records it, which provide a sequence of events that prod us to interpret its significance. As with speculative design, objects must be situated in a context; moreover, such contextualization is established through media that can convey a narrative, namely photography, film, and pseudo-documentary. Critical design is characterized by its dark humour. It works through juvenalian forms of satire where antithesis, obscenity, and violence are used to engage the user through prolepsis and allegory. The work in this category focuses on social, cultural, and ethical implications of design objects and practice, using design practice as a tool to challenge norms. The critical approach taken is more violent, savage, and pointed in its critique than in examples of speculative and associative design.

In my practice, I have explored the behavioural and psychological effects that result from the use and misuse of mobile phones though the project *Consequences of Use* (2006). The project is a critique of instrumental theories of technology as a neutral entity and takes a substantive view of mobile communication technologies. *Consequences of Use* explores messier contexts of use inquiring into the agency of the mobile phone and resulting anxiety, addiction, and violence. One aspect of the project, *First Aid for Users Suffering a Loss of Connection*, explores technology as human extension. Rather than considering the physical integration of technology into the body, the project

Figure 5.8 Matt Malpass, *First Aid for Users Suffering a Loss of Connection*, 2006.

considers the psychological link between user and mobile phone technologies. It questions the need to treat a loss of connection as we would an injury. The design provides means for the suffering user to synchronize lost technology with emergency devices on which you can download a saved profile reconnecting you to your digital world.

In *Design for Fragile Personalities in Anxious Times* (2004–05), Dunne and Raby celebrate humans as contradictory, complex, and psychologically flawed. Obscenity, violence, and understatement are used as satiric techniques. They play down fear of nuclear annihilation, proposing products that condition the user to become comfortable with the idea. The project has a serious function as it is designed to explore the concept of fear and anxiety through a targeted conversation with mental health workers. Dunne and Raby's *Placebo* project shifts the role of design from affirmation of norms to inquiry. Explicitly 'taking conceptual design beyond the gallery into everyday life' (Dunne and Raby 2002, 11), eight prototypes with relations to the electromagnetic properties of technology were produced. 'Made from MDF and usually one other specialist material, the objects are purposefully diagrammatic and vaguely familiar. They are open ended enough to prompt stories but not to bewilder' (Dunne and Raby 2002, 11). The objects were placed in users' homes and as a result, personal narratives and emerging behaviours were exposed as relationships with the objects that developed over time. Narrative stories around placebo objects were developed by which attention was drawn to unseen conditions in the domestic environment, and by extension the opportunities and threats that environment might offer. In *Is This Your Future*, a critical design experiment commissioned by the Science Museum, London Dunne and Raby explore the future of energy production by presenting a collection of hypothetical products to explore the ethical, cultural, and social impact factors. Photographic scenarios were used to communicate a set of values driven by social, as well as technological, changes. The scenarios included biofuel created from human waste. The satire is at once very subtle and very simple; however, Dunne and Raby's proposal is not at all modest and an excellent example of critical design working through juvenalian satire. They suggest using child labour to produce energy and take responsibility for their own energy consumption. The project works through understatement and obscenity, playing down child labour and tapping into the technical possibilities of using human waste to power domestic consumer products implying that human beings can or might be transformed from fuel consumers to energy providers. Like much critical design, the project is more diverse and often much more polemic in its tone than speculative and associative design.

Noam Toran's project *Objects for Lonely Men* is classified as critical design. It tells the story of a man so obsessed with Jean-Luc Godard's *A Bout de Souffle* that he builds a tray that reflects the physical language of the film. The tray contains a series of objects that the man interacts with. The objects include a mannequin head which resembles Jean Seberg – the female lead, a gun, a hat similar to the one Jean-Paul Belmondo wears in the movie, telephone, Herald Tribune newspaper, sunglasses, ashtray, steering wheel, rear-view mirror, and a pack of Gitanes non-filtered cigarettes. The project addresses the influence of film on identity and fantasy. It explores how objects often mediate these fantasies. The work uses products and film to investigate anomalies in human behaviour, reflecting dissent towards imposed social conformity. In the project, there is a darkly humorous conflict established by techniques of antithesis. Toran denotes behaviour that sits outside social conformity but is presented in a scenario of use that is understated and the practice appears relatively normal. Through this, Toran aims to question the systems that organize society.

This theme is explored further in *Desire Management* (2005). *Desire Management* is a film comprising five sequences where objects are used as vehicles for dissident behaviour. Based on real testimonials and news reports, the design device attempts to reveal the inherent need for expression and identity formation in the face of conformist society. The objects afford strange experiences and satisfy specific psychological needs, for example, an airline hostess with a unique relationship to turbulence, the owner of a mysterious box which men ritually visit to look inside, an elderly man who enjoys being

Figure 5.9 *Desire Management*/© Noam Toran. Courtesy of the artist.

vacuumed, a couple who engage in baseball-driven fantasies, and a man who is forced by his partner to cry into a strange device. Through the project, Toran positions the domestic space as the last private frontier and a space for non-conformist expression in a conformist material culture.

Onkar Kular's *Hari and Parker* (2007) is another example of critical design. Kular conceived the characters Hari and Parker for *The Science of Spying* exhibition at the Science Museum, London, 2007. Kular sets up an imagined alternate reality in which children are recruited to spy for the government and are conditioned and helped along by Hari, a rabbit and Parker, a bear. Kular developed a line of children's products featuring the characters. Hari has microphone ears that intercept text messaging and Parker's nose hides a camera, while his paw is a fingerprint scanner to aid children in committing acts of domestic surveillance. The project works through understatement and caricature, playing down the increasing presence of surveillance and information exchange in contemporary society.

Before Kular, Vexed Generation was exploring similar themes commenting on, amongst other things, a culture of surveillance through design practice. Thorpe and Hunter conceived the *Vexed Parka* to meet both the practical needs and political concerns of the urban generation in 1990s London. Introduced in 1995, the designers considered personal safety but also addressed civil liberties, street protest, and CCTV surveillance through the design. Violence and understatement are used as satiric response in the form of a parka that obscures identity and protects vulnerable parts of the body against heavy-handed police

Figure 5.10 Adam Thorpe and Joe Hunter Vexed Generation, *Vexed Parka*, 1995.

strategies to detain protestors. The design is informed by a detailed study of these strategies and responsive to them in the features designed into the garment.

Thorpe and Hunter's critical practice moves beyond commentary and generating public debate into a territory of active participation in activism. Their *Vexed Parka* moved from a critical object reflecting the state of policing in London to become bought and ultimately used as functioning urban armour and as a symbol of protest and dissent in the face of heavy-handed policing.

Design practice as satire

The examples discussed throughout this chapter establish their critique through a form of satiric design. Satire has long been used as a device to offer critique, but it also provides a provocative lens by which to examine design's forms of critical practice. To reiterate what was introduced in chapter 3, satire, with its established theoretical foundation, diminishes a subject by making it ridiculous and evoking attitudes of amusement, contempt, scorn, or indignation towards it. In design's various critical practices, satire functions as constructive social criticism. In achieving this, the designers use wit as an instrument to afford critical reflection and engage a user audience through humour. In this way, critical design practice highlights the vices, abuses, and shortcomings found in orthodox product design, while holding scientific developments or sociocultural conditions up to ridicule. At its most strident, this is done with the intent of shaming individuals, the discipline, or even society itself to reflect and ultimately work towards the improvement of a situation.

In classical terms, two major forms of satire are employed in critical design practice: *juvenalian* and *horatian*. Juvenalian satire is often political, savage, and pointed; it works through narrative techniques of antithesis, obscenity, and violence. Horatian satire is less savage as it identifies folly and works through paradoxical techniques of burlesque, colloquialism, exaggeration, and anticlimax.[2]

Associative design works through horatian satire. In the horatian approach, the designer takes either an existing work that was created with a serious purpose, or an object with reputable characteristics, and then makes the work look ridiculous by infusing it with incongruous ideas. This is achieved by presenting it in inappropriate forms, remaking it by using inappropriate materials or by subverting the context in which it might be used. The work parodies design to construct criticism. Parody is a composition that imitates the serious manner and characteristic features of a particular work, or the distinctive style of its maker. It then applies the imitation to a lowly or comically inappropriate subject. It is a variety of burlesque, a form of satire characterized by ridiculous exaggeration. A serious subject may be treated frivolously or a frivolous subject seriously.

Speculative and critical design work through juvenalian satire. By working through narrative forms of allegory, exaggeration, antithesis, obscenity, and violence, juvenalian satire is 'darker' than horatian satire. In this respect, the juvenalian designer approaches their work by attacking perceived errors in logic or thinking, and as such tries to evoke contempt, shock, and righteous indignation in the mind of the user audience.

Accordingly, speculative design works through mechanisms of exaggeration, distortion, and allegory. In this use of satire, however, recognition must precede correction. Recognition on the users' part is afforded through the designer's understanding of allegory; the latter constructs narratives of use around technological products and the application of new science. This satire is achieved by changing the perspective on a condition or situation. By separating something from its ordinary context, speculative design emphasizes some aspects of the problem and plays down others through methods of exaggeration or understatement.

Finally, critical design works in a somewhat different manner, relying on antithesis, counterproposition, and allegory. The narratives developed here depict scenarios as a means to visualizing alternatives. Critical designers evoke dark humour, while using polemic narratives employing forms of obscenity and violence.

Certain techniques lend themselves easily to satire because they can contain a measure of both wit and humour, and the necessary satiric association. Among them are exaggeration, distortion, understatement, innuendo, and allegory. A brief example of each of these will help illustrate the versatility of the satiric method and the ways the satirist designers presents their criticism.

Exaggeration is one of the most commonly used techniques, since the depiction of an extreme or blatantly vicious case is one of the best ways to get the target user to recognize, or admit, that an issue or problem exists at all – recognition must precede correction. The designer satirist brings his description of what is wrong with a situation to its logical extreme, exaggerating by overemphasis in order to make the unseeing see and the seeing-but-complacent oppose. This approach is evident in the work of Ball and Naylor, Gamper, and Bey discussed previously in the chapter.

Understatement is the converse of exaggeration and is useful in cases where the problem faced is already so great that it can hardly be exaggerated. The mention of the problem by understatement serves to call attention to the true degree of the problem. This approach is evident in the work of Jones's *Chicken Factory* and *Sea Chair* discussed previously. The projects address severe environmental concerns and practices through a commentary delivered through humble understated quotidian objects.

Distortion is commonly used in critical practice. Distortion effectively changes the perspective of a condition or event by isolation, that is, the separation from its ordinary surroundings, or by stressing some aspects and deemphasizing others. This is most prominent in speculative design and the projects discussed above, where science is taken out of the laboratory and materialized through object and scenarios of use applied in everyday settings and domestic environments.

Innuendo and insinuation is a valuable tool for the satirist designer because it allows them to implicate a target by a completely indirect attack as exemplified in the work of Onkar Kular *Harry and Parker.*

Allegory is the final element I will include here. Designers typically use allegories as rhetorical devices that convey their position through symbolic figures, actions, imagery, and events that together create the moral, ethical, or political meaning that they wish to convey. The critique is more likely to be remembered in the allegory because of the vehicle of the story and its use of physical realities such as the use of behaviours, objects, interactions, and the people used to represent the concepts presented. This is most prominent in speculative design and the development, visualization, and communication of the extrinsic narratives that typify examples of the practice.

The uses of narrative

In this satiric critical design practice, a quality of narrative is always essential. Fundamentally, it describes the use of storytelling techniques to pass comment or inquire through the actions of designing. Narratives of use situate the product in a context that allows the user to understand and engage with the design and further its satiric forms.

Relying on a subtle form of satire, associative design uses a form of embedded narrative. The object offers a laconic criticism. In this context, objects stand alone and are rarely contextualized by external medium e.g. writing, supporting images, and film. The commentary is embedded in the object through the materials used and the form the object takes. An embedded narrative is possible because of the subversion of familiar typology and collective understanding as in the example of Ralph Ball and Maxine Naylor, *24 Star Generic Office Chair.*

Because of their provisional and unfamiliar characteristics, many objects of speculative design require a detailed supporting narrative to establish their use. This is established through scenario building where objects and technologies are situated in contexts of use. Through technocratic visualization, for example in Dunne and Raby's *Foragers* project narrative, meanings are constructed through specially made devices. But the unfamiliar can also shape narrative by assigning unusual objects with descriptive names, for example, as in Alexandra Daisy Ginsburg's *Growth Assembly*, Carole Collet's *Biolace*, and Tobie Kerridge's *Biojewellery*. Sometimes, too, the use of external media such as film, photography, and performance supplement and contextualize these objects. In this respect, the critique is established through a synthesis of objects and contextualizing material.

Critical design operates in a similar way by also making use of film, photography, and narrative naming, thus establishing an extrinsic narrative to establish contexts of use. Here, however, a topic is criticized because it falls short of some standard that the designer desires that it should reach. This is expressed through a critical narrative that ridicules or otherwise attacks conditions needing reformation. In 2006, Björn Franke presented *Traces of an Imaginary Affair*, a device that could imitate scratch marks made on the back by an invented lover. Such an object might allow the user to self-harm in order to feel self-worth. The design relies on the understanding that self-harm is wrong. But it also challenges such assumptions through juxtaposition, tension, and contradiction, imagining how harming might actually instil value and worth. It is in the difference between the proposed scenario and societal convention that critique is established and debate provoked.

Horatian satire – and therefore associative design – primarily operates through narratives constructed through parody: familiar forms are parodied and subverted. The critique can be embedded in the objects because of the user familiarity with the objects. Juvenalian satire, and therefore speculative and critical design, works through narratives constructed through allegory. The proposed objects are unfamiliar and require contextualizing with supporting information.

Rationality and ambiguity

Ambiguity is also useful because the intention can always be denied, but it also serves to make the satiric comparison more pointed by making difficult any distinction between the target and the object to which it is compared. Things are presented 'vague' so that we wonder 'why' and 'what if?' Ambiguity is therefore used as a clear accusation to provoke questions. Any construction capable of conveying a double meaning is likely to be employed in satire, since multiple meanings form the basis of much of satire.

Objects of associative design are rational, familiar, and understandable in their own right, but subverting familiar typologies and making these objects strange create an ambiguity of context. Martino Gamper, for example, remakes seats using parts of accessible chairs. He constructs series of unique seats that also remain functional. This form of critique is useful in spurring people to approach a particular design with an open mind and, more generally, get them to question the assumptions they may hold about the chair or other objects.

Speculative design is concerned with developing technology or science and projects possibilities. Often these innovations are yet to be appropriated into everyday life. Because of this, its objects are non-rational – they are not immediately understandable or assimilated into the collective imaginary; the object and its use are dependent on the fabrication of an external narrative to contextualize it and make sense of the object and its context of use. While the aim of constructed narratives is to make sense of the object, some level of ambiguity is still necessary in order to provoke debate. Therefore, the focus in speculative design is on creating uncertainties about the information delivered through the design and its supporting narrative, while at the same time positioning it as an object of product design. The purpose of this may be merely to make the design work seem mysterious or impressionistic, but more importantly it can also compel people to join in the work of making sense of the design. Auger's *Smell+: Dating and Genetic Compatibility Smell Blind Date*, for example, reminds us of research into the role and potential uses that might capitalize on recent discoveries of pheromones and other chemical scents.

Critical design objects are also non-rational. Here the object is placed in context through mechanisms of narrative storytelling and allegory. Relational ambiguity is used, leading the users to consider new beliefs and values and ultimately question their own attitudes. The relational aspects of the design create conditions for a personal projection of imagination and values onto a design. This allows objects to become psychological mirrors for people, pushing them to question their values and activities. Dunne and Raby's *Is This Your Future: Poo Lunch Box*, discussed in Chapter 4, forces us to imagine tapping into the technical possibilities of using human waste to power domestic consumer products; this provokes us to question our own position, beliefs, and reservations relative to the proposition.

Towards a taxonomy of critical practices

Rationality, narrative, and satire each interlink. The more rational an object is, the more laconic the critique and the critical move is established through horatian satire. Where there is a need for an extrinsic allegoric narrative, the objects are less rational and the critical move established through juvenalian forms of satire. The design methods used in critical design practice and the methods of classification are summarized in Table 5.1.

Table 5.1 Taxonomic Matrix. The matrix illustrates the relationship between the types of practice and the methods used. It shows how the design methods relate to the type of ambiguity, the type of object rationality, the type of satire.

Practice	Method: Definition	Type of Satire: Satiric Mechanism	Type of Ambiguity	Object Rationality
Associative Design	Cut up: When one or more objects are cut up or reassembled to exaggerate their properties and give new meaning Context transfer: When one object is taken out of context and placed into another	Horatian: Burlesque Parody Reductio ad absurdum	Ambiguity of context	Rational: Familiar archetype
Speculative Design	Hybridity: One archetype is integrated with another archetype. This might take the form of two objects but also practices. For example, technology that exists in a laboratory context is placed in a quotidian setting. Technocratic visualization: Technocracy is a wide-ranging visual system that is legitimized by specific reference to scientific expertise. The science rationalizes the proposition.	Horatian / Juvenalian: Allegory Anticlimax Distortion Exaggeration Narrative	Ambiguity of Information	
Critical Design	Extrinsic narrative: A narrative is established to situate the object. Questions are raised in the difference between 'reality' and the materiality proposed through the object and its narrative of use.	Juvenalian: Allegory Antithesis Obscenity Violence Prolepsis	Relational ambiguity	Non-rational: Unfamiliar archetype

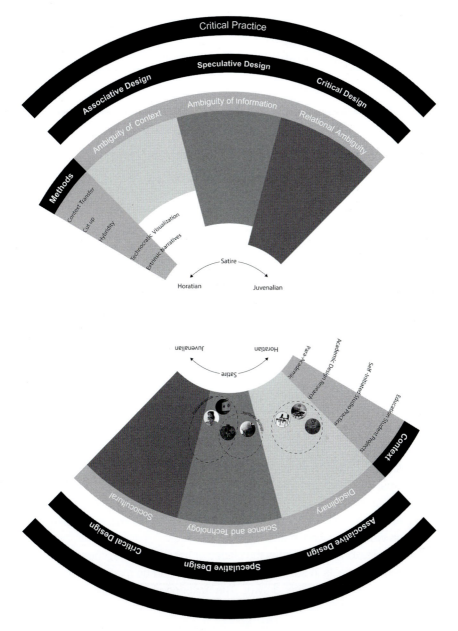

Figure 5.11 Taxonomy of critical practice: The model can be used to map examples according to the methods, tactics, contexts of operation, and type of critical practice.

These conditions afford the capacity to structure associative, speculative, and critical design into a taxonomic space as shown in Figure 5.11. By considering if a design project can be categorized as associative, speculative, or critical design and in identifying the context in which it was carried out, this model can be used in a number of ways to map critical practices, allowing us to view relationships between examples of practice and chart their trajectories.

The taxonomy as an analytical tool

The taxonomy therefore presents a theoretical apparatus to engage with the field of critical practice. I'll begin by introducing the components of the taxonomy.

The top half of the model shows the categories of practice. The three practices are structured alongside each other, from right to left: associative design through speculative design to critical design. The type of ambiguity that each of the practices operates by is shown, for example ambiguity of context, ambiguity of information, or relational ambiguity. The design methods that are used to build ambiguity into the design work and establish the system of use are also illustrated, for example, 'cutup' and 'extrinsic narrative'.

Moving from associative design through speculative design to critical design, the characteristics of the objects become less rational and the objects are typically less familiar. Because of this, more of an external narrative is required in speculative design to situate the object in its system of use, and even more so in critical design. Moving from associative design to critical design there is also a scale of satire ranging from horatian in associative design through to juvenalian in critical design.

The three categories of practice in the top half of the taxonomic model are reflected in the bottom half. This half of the model is sectioned according to the context that a project is carried out from. These contexts are studio projects, education, academic design research, and para-academic contexts. This allows examples of associative, speculative, and critical design to be plotted against the context in which they were carried out.

The visual taxonomy facilitates the placement of associative, speculative, and critical design projects in such a way that projects can be mapped, contrasted, and trajectories of practice drawn. The taxonomy in its visual dimension presents an illustrative summary of the relationship between the three categories of practice introduced in this chapter structured by the methods and tactics employed in practice.

Applications of the taxonomy

The model can be used as a model to map numerous examples of practice from numerous designers. In *Mapping the Terrain*, projects can be plotted according to the type of practice and where they are carried out. The model can be used to plot *individual designers' projects*. It can illustrate what projects a designer is involved in at any one time and if there is a clear correlation of activity in any of the three types of practice. Extending this, the taxonomy can be used as a background to discuss *trajectories of practice* by plotting projects by the date when they were carried out. This might be used to plot a single designer or studio's practice or may include examples from a number of practitioners. The model can be used to identify *clusters of activity* and trends in projects at a specific time. Clustering a designer's body of work or a larger community's work allows questions to be asked of why that activity was so prominent at a specific time. This might be cross-referenced with other factors, for example funding themes, theoretical trends, or sociotechnical and political considerations. The model can be used to *compare* design and draw comparisons between practitioners and projects. For example, it can be used to analyse the content of an exhibition or works documented on a designer's website. The taxonomy offers theoretical apparatus to understand, analyse, and discuss examples of critical design practice and how and where they operate.

Conclusions

This chapter has defined three specific types of critical design practice. The discussion outlined methods by which these practices operate. Common to the field is the use of satire, rationality, and narrative to engage and offer critique. The purpose of critical design concurrent with the function of satire is constructive criticism, using wit as an instrument to affect critical reflection. There is no satire without critique and humour is a powerful tool of engagement. But this critique is contingent on reading the objects of critical practice as objects of design. These are, therefore, always contextualized and rationalized with a narrative of use.

Critical practices in design today are in flux. Moreover, if design must establish an intellectual stance of its own, we must explore its critical turn more fully. Above all, we must perceive how design responds to disciplinary, scientific, or social concerns. This chapter has examined how satire in design can relate to the type of ambiguity used in each of the three types of critical practice. By extension, it also helps us understand how rational an object is, and how it contains a narrative.

Satire, ambiguity, and rationality relate to each other and all help to characterize and differentiate between associative, critical, and speculative design practice. The relationships between the categories of critical design, the design methods used, and the methods of classification are summarized. These are structured into a taxonomic space that offers theoretical apparatus to engage with the field of critical design practice. Throughout the chapter, the taxonomy has been populated with examples of critical design projects to illustrate the model's application as an analytical tool and apparatus for discussion. To conclude, the taxonomy provides a means to map the territory of critical design practice, offering observers of the practice a territory to analyse and critique. The implications of the taxonomy and its application are detailed in the following and concluding chapter.

6

CRITICAL DESIGN PRACTICE AND ITS DISCIPLINARY CONTRIBUTION

In this book, I have introduced examples of critical design practice and discussed the tactics used to establish a critical move through product and industrial design. I have outlined a brief history of the practice, theoretical approaches that inform critical practice and explored, through the categorization of associative, speculative, and critical design, where critical practice engages and critiques matters of concern familiar to the product design discipline, and those matters of concern that are not so familiar. By means of a conclusion, this chapter sets out an argument for the disciplinary contribution that critical design practice makes.

Summary

The discussion in Chapter 2 described how the term 'critical design' appeared some twenty years ago in the design research community as a particular approach to human-computer interaction. Referring to a longer tradition of critical approaches in product design and architecture, it was meant to re-establish alternative views on product and interface design, telling stories about human values and behaviour that were neglected in commercial product design. The discussion charted a history from Radical Design in the Italian tradition; Anti-Design, New Design, and Conceptual Design in the German and Dutch traditions; and critical practice in HCI, Interaction Design, and Critical Technical Practice. Associative, speculative, and critical design projects carried out today are heavily influenced by the methods and approaches developed in these preceding practices and are influenced by the anti-capitalist, anti-commercial, ethically led, and activist ideologies that informed these earlier modes of critical practice.

The discussion showed how contemporary examples of critical design practice are informed by aesthetic principles established in the 1960s and 1970s and how these approaches have been practiced throughout the lineage of critical practice. To illustrate this, Peter Cook's Archigram *Instant City Airships* was compared to Brendan Walker's *Chromo 11 Air Life Seat Belts* and Superstudio's *Monumento Continuo* alongside Dunne and Raby's *United Micro Kingdoms Digitarians*. These examples show how the design language in critical design practice today is informed by work produced over forty years ago. The benefit of looking at the history of critical design practice came from identifying design methods used to establish the critical move through design. The review of precedents identified 'cutup', 'context transfer', 'hybridity', and 'technocratic visualization' as methods used to build ambiguity into objects. These methods are used in contemporary examples of practice and from a theoretical perspective, they offer a means to differentiate between the examples of associative, speculative, and critical design and are used to inform the structure of the taxonomy presented in Chapter 5.

Chapter 3 focused on the discourse surrounding critical design since the development and popularization of the term 'c.1993'. It described the use of product design to address various social, technical, scientific, and disciplinary concerns. The discussion outlined the theoretical perspectives that ground critical design practice outlining the perspectives of Dunne (1997), Redström and Hällnass (2002a, 2002b), and Ball and Naylor (2006). It focused on the 'aesthetics of use', 'correspondence and context', 'para-functionality', and the 'post-optimal object'. It described the instrumental use of 'ambiguity as a resource for design' and established that designing ambiguity into the object – in its appearance and its use – is instrumental in establishing the critical move through product design.

The type of ambiguity designed into critical design work was identified as another means to differentiate between examples of critical design practice. With reference to Gaver, Beaver, and Benford (2003), three types of ambiguity were identified. Associative design works through 'ambiguity of context', speculative design works through 'ambiguity of information', and critical design through 'relational ambiguity'. In practical terms, the discussion set out in Chapter 3 illustrated the sensitivity required when designing ambiguity into objects as a means to spark debate, engagement, or to establish the critical move. For associative, critical, or speculative design to work, the objects designed must be seen as design objects. Put simply, too odd and they will not work, too strange and the designs will not engage the user. The work produced – be it a lone object or an object contextualized by an extrinsic narrative established through a film or some other medium – should always relate back to quotidian conditions. Good examples of critical design practice tap into users' familiar understanding of objects of use. They subvert the understanding between users and object, essentially exploiting the evocative characteristics of designed objects. This creates a dilemma of interpretation afforded by the contradiction, tension, and juxtaposition of an object of use and the subversion of users' conventional understanding of how that object might be used. It is in this tension, in this dilemma of interpretation, that questions are asked and channels of discourse are opened. This function of critical design practice is useful when trying to develop an understanding of how the designers establish inquiry through design and frame the practice as research.

Where this dilemma of interpretation is established using 'ambiguity', 'design fictions', and 'strangely familiar' objects, through methods commonly associated with art practice, it is all too easy to see the work as something other than product design. Because of these characteristics, critical design practice is often subject to art discourse, critique, and gallery circulation. The assertion made by the designers, that the work *is* design, *is* important since the power of critical design practice lies in its objects being seen as product design.

As a method, strategy, or theoretical perspective, critical design has been widely interpreted. It has shown how it has been appropriated in an increasing number of student projects and adopted by many trying to find a label for what they do. With this has come a sporadic analysis of the field that often discusses the work with reference to its proximity to art practice. The book has questioned some analysis of the practice that comes from exhibition and curation perspectives. In this context, appraisal can be accused of being unrepresentative and affirmative. This was exemplified in Antonelli's account of Catts and Zurr's work during the *Design and the Elastic Mind* exhibition that was astutely challenged by Cogdell (2009) in her *Design Issues* review of it. The discussion revealed how dominant criticism and analysis of critical design is often grounded in perspectives rooted in art and visual culture discourses. The discussion identified the criticism of critical design practice and the barriers that exist to seeing critical design practice as product design.

The focus here set up one of the main arguments and concerns in this book: the danger of critical design practice being seen as a form or quasi art or as a form of design entertainment enjoyed for its humour or novelty rather than for its insight. Critical design practice needs to avoid this by inviting commentary and critique of the practice. The first thing to address in aiming to establish this design-centric analysis is the barriers that exist to seeing critical design as a form of product design. Most clearly, this is the question of critical design practice's proximity to art. Even the most open-minded design professionals and researchers question if critical design operates as product design because it does not serve to solve problems through highly resolved objects or innovative systems design. Considering the 'isn't it just art?' question, a concept of function based on optimization and efficiency was identified as the measure used by many to differentiate between objects of art and design.

In an attempt to move the discussion away from the 'art question', the common perception of function, or more accurately 'practical functionality', was challenged and a concept of function conceived beyond efficiency and optimization was presented. The discussion here drew on literature from design theory, but also from other disciplines that engage with objects, form, and materiality. Archaeologists have an interesting and useful take when attempting to re-conceptualize function. Ligo (1984) and Schiffer (1992) extend function beyond efficiency into more social and even existential contexts. Material culture perspectives also contribute and should be considered in any attempt to reframe function. Miller (1987) was again useful in his call to think about a more open interpretation and the sociological perspective (Shove, Watson, and Ingram 2007) and brought current thinking on practice-orientated design into play.

Just as these perspectives support the rationality of function, the discussion identified designers and scholars who advocate a socially constructed and dynamic function of, and for, objects. The discussion showed how Brandes, Stich, and Wender (2009), Kroes (2010), and Fisher and Shipton (2010) suggest forms of use that, despite the designer's intent, function will always emerge in use. This perspective is shared by Mazé (2007) in her thesis exploring the 'temporal form of interaction', Wilkie (2010) in his 'user assemblages', and Niedderer (2004, 2006) in her category of the 'performative object'.

The discussion located how function can be considered in a context of critical design practice. It showed that an object's function is open to the interpretation by the user and the intention of the designer. In short, function is an ill-defined and open concept; it extends beyond optimization and efficiency into social existential and cultural contexts, and therefore it provides insufficient grounds to frame critical design practice in art discourse. The reality is that things are more complex than a simple design/art dichotomy. In a context of critical design practice, if both user and designer are willing to see the object as a functioning design object, then the object does function as an object of design and should be discussed as such.

This discussion of function was useful because it established that critical design practice operates through a system of 'rhetorical use'. Rhetorical use was introduced as a form of symbolic and intellectual use. This use is afforded through the designer's projection of the object in material form, and imagination on the part of the user. Rhetorical use is just as legitimate as practical use.

Accepting rhetorical use as a legitimate form of use counters arguments based on the claim that critical design is not useful and does not function. There is more to the function of designed objects than just practical considerations. Through this proposition, I challenge the reader to overcome the modernist doctrine inherent in 'form follows function' and by doing this, overcome one of the biggest barriers to seeing and talking about critical design as product design. An open concept of function and use, as advocated by those cited above, shifts focus beyond aesthetic questions to open critical design practice up to a more design-centric analysis. An analysis where questions can be asked of the object, which orient around contexts and systems of use, the practices that might situate the object or the behaviours that might emerge as a result of engaging with, and using the critical design object.

The discussion in Chapter 4 outlined the need for apparatus to facilitate discussion into critical design practice. The premise here is that models make sense of things. A model of the practice that illustrates its position in relation to other forms of design practice and places it in a disciplinary context, developed from a product design perspective, might engage a broader discussion of the practice and by extension advance the theoretical foundation of the practice. The discussion detailed work carried out in this vain. Sanders's (2006) 'evolving map of design research and practice' places critical design in a design research context; Walker's (2010) positioning of critical design as 'fundamental research' showed how critical design functions as research in a design process and as a means of ideation. A rhizomic model of the field and its reach was identified in *Design* Act (2009). Mazé positioned critical design practice amongst examples of socially responsible design practice, participatory design, and co-design practices that are political by nature and orientate around active critical participation. Considering how others have explored and conceptualized critical design practice, the chapter introduced a characteristic of critical design practice that differentiates it from other forms of socially and politically engaged practices. There is a trend to discuss critical design alongside other forms of socially engaged participatory and co-design practices (Bülmann 2008; Sanders and Stappers 2008; Design Act 2009). Arguably, critical design practice as it has been described in this book, differs from these practices in that it functions as an authoritative form of product design. The 'critical' designer performs as author and critic, and although this has changed slightly in speculative design practice where designers frequently collaborate with experts in scientific contexts, there remains an authorship over the work and often a polemic thread is engendered in the design and narratives of use. In short, the designer takes a critical position through the medium of product and industrial design. Such a view of the field differentiates it from other forms of socially responsible or responsive forms of design practice, participatory, or co-design which are characterized by the redistribution of power in making design decisions from the designer to the stakeholder users. However, I recognize that these practices are also critical of prevailing orthodoxy and are having deterritorializing effects on the role of the designer and what constitutes product design practice today.

The taxonomy presented in Chapter 5 works to illustrate the diversity in critical design practice. It shows how critical design practice broadly constitutes three types of practice: associative, critical, and speculative design. This conceptualization positions the colloquial and popularly understood view of critical design in a broader context of critical design practice. Critical design has a history in associative design and a future in speculative design. All three forms of practice exist today in contemporary product design practice. The taxonomy contextualizes critical design practice in three ways. First, it is used to show the contexts engendered in the practice, the disciplinary, science, and technology, or sociocultural project focus. Second, it shows where a project is carried out (the operating context). Academic design research, the gallery system, and various studio practices were identified as contexts that facilitate the practice. The range of examples discussed show how the practice is closely linked to design schools and the academy. These spaces provide the freedom from the restraints imposed by industry and produce another form of capital, epistemic, and human capital. This illustrated the importance of the institution to the practice. Third, it shows how the practice operates through satire and methods used to establish a critical narrative through design. Satiric design was identified as salient and is useful because, as a concept, it addresses questions about *how* critical design is done. Notably, critical design practice functions through the marriage of design principles and satire. Inseparable from any definition of satire is critique and corrective purpose, expressed through a critical mode that ridicules or otherwise challenges conditions needing reformation in the opinion of the critical designer as satirist.

The taxonomy, by discussing key theoretical concepts that inform critical design and defining categories of practice, design methods, and contexts of operation, and structuring them into a taxonomic space, offers theoretical apparatus to engage with the field. It provides designers a territory to operate from and observers of the practice a territory to analyse and critique.

Throughout these chapters, I have hoped to illustrate that critical design is a rich and important form of design practice, capable of inquiry, commentary, debate, and provocation in social, scientific, and disciplinary matters of concern. I have hoped to articulate that this field warrants analysis in order for it to continue in its development and make a valuable contribution to product design. I have hoped to provide a theoretical apparatus by which to engage an audience in the discourse of critical design practice and offer a point of entry by developing the terminology and laying down definitions around which the practice can be discussed. The premise here is that to develop the practice more people from outside critical design need to engage and challenge it.

Challenging disciplinary orthodoxy

Through a discussion of the history, theory, and practice of critical design, we have seen how it offers an alternative application for the product and industrial design skillset, and its design process and methods, to that of the commercially orientated mainstream product design practice. However, common to both critical and mainstream practice is the execution of design judgment honed and exercised through the designer's practice, where tool-based creativity and making – in some form or another – is at the core of the practice. Because critical practice – in the guises of associative, speculative, and critical design – utilizes skills that are core to mainstream industrial design, it contributes to product and industrial design as a discipline by demonstrating the application of designerly skill, judgment, and process in broad contexts. It works to extend the purview of what product design is, and what can be considered within product and industrial design's disciplinary remit. We have seen throughout that even though critical design projects are carried out in conceptual frames where the objects remain at the scale of one off provocations, critical designers attribute importance to the processes, methods, and principles of industrial design. This is illustrated by how the design work produced relates back to a quotidian understanding of objects afforded through the user's familiarity with form and forms of interaction. The designers leverage the user's familiarity to engage audiences in thought and discussion around the themes engendered in the design work. In many of the examples, we see a high finish in the designed object, carefully considered production, and assembly and the utilization of models and prototypes that are situated in detailed visual scenarios that depict how these objects are used.

In critical design practice, the designers value the same rules and expectations in the production of work, as they would if working on a commercial project. There is attention to form and contexts of use. The tools and design methods applied are equally relevant and applicable in both forms of practice. Both forms map the problem context, survey the horizon, and are concerned with the future. Both critical and mainstream designers imagine objects and the scenarios that these objects will live in; they are concerned with affecting change and intervening in the future – at some scale.

So, as with a commercial brief where an understanding of context and circumstances of use are absolutely everything, where the project's success hinges on the appropriate identification and management of the design problem in context through the identification and analysis of insight, and the translation of this insight into an appropriate and relevant design response, critical design practice honours the same design traditions and the same reasoning in the design work that is expected from orthodox design practice.

Critical design practice does not function in a market context, this does not however, provide a caveat for shortcuts in the design process. It does not provide caveat for the absence of the design reasoning and iterative engagement expected of any good design work. The analysis, reasoning, judgment, iteration, testing, and creative output expected of any design process is paramount and should be present in the critical design process. When this is the case, projects are successful. There are many examples of designers claiming work as critical design, using critical and speculative design as a handy label to hide behind when the work does not come from a critical position inherent in the designer and is not the product of a rigorous process.

In a critical design project, design methods and the production of design work are positioned as a system of critical thought. Rather than using other mediums, critical designers value the reflective and iterative processes that are fundamental to industrial design practice. They emphasize the processes of designing in order to articulate a position and develop understanding through making, tool-based creativity, and the dissemination of process and products of design. Amidst attitudes of dissatisfaction and frustration with the status quo – in disciplinary, technological, and societal contexts – there is a collective refusal by the critical designers discussed throughout this book to abandon product design practice. It would be all too easy to frame the projects as other forms of creative practice, but the refusal to do so affords critical design agency to offer a criticism from within design practice. Within the examples discussed, there is a belief that the function of product and industrial design can be extended into provocative realms and that design has the potential to open up new avenues of discourse and reflect on the principles and values inherent in product design.

While dissident in character, the refusal to abandon the product design discipline through the application of design language, methods, and principles, offers a valuable contribution to the discipline. The critique of the discipline, through the subversion of disciplinary traditions, adds a new practice of values. This fits with a concept of critique where critique is a practice that not only suspends judgment but also offers a new practice of values based on that very suspension (2002xx). In establishing this critique, the designers aim to extend the purview of the discipline and what product design is capable of addressing beyond fiscal and technological drivers. This suspension of conventional market, user, and technologically driven values paradoxically adds value to product and industrial design. Critical design practice therefore has an agonistic relationship to orthodox product design, a relationship based on a plurality and advocacy. When critical and mainstream design are seen as complementary fields operating constructively in an agonistic relationship, critical design practice advances the product discipline. It offers the means to look inward at the processes and principles of design rather than passively accept normative practice and hegemony. It serves to challenge a 'business as usual' model within the discipline and profession. The role here is not to undermine or subvert the profession, but to challenge it and drive it forward as a thoughtful and reflective agent. Moreover, engaging fields, practices, and issues beyond perceived disciplinary silos and boundaries take the industrial designer into new territories of operation. This creates opportunities for knowledge generation, collaboration, and importantly, the possibility of new professional roles for product and industrial designers i.e.

working in contexts such as medical ethics, synthetic biology, politics, and the plethora of other contexts that critical and speculative design are engaging with.

Looking at this pragmatically might mean more jobs for designers as it offers a potential to do design work in contexts that sit outside a saturated job market – it moves the designer beyond the design consultancy and the in-house studio towards a role for the designer in think tanks, policy-making, technological research centres, third-sector organizations, and academic research centres – to name just a few facilitating contexts derived from the examples discussed throughout this book.

An extended role for industrial design: Discipline, science, and society

Critical designers exercise disciplinary confidence. They trust and value the application of industrial design and how it contributes to problem contexts considered outside mainstream design. This activity extends the scope and agency of today's industrial designer into new contexts of operation and engagement. The designers share the belief that product design is more than a profession, more than an agent of capital, and is a powerful medium, language, and process through which to make comment and engage inquiry. The affective and relational character of the work opens channels of discourse on and around the object. Design used in this way works as part of a research process. Research in this sense sits in opposition to positivist research methods that aim to present facts, which as often as they contribute to knowledge, close down avenues of inquiry. The ability to provoke discussion on an object and to engage a public has an instrumental application in the research context. In this context, the designs function as probes offering means to make sense of emerging science, comment on societal concerns, and construct publics around these matters of concern. Galloway poignantly describes this:

> Since facts seem to end debates, and design seems to open them up, our greatest chance for critical intervention arise in our engagement of shared concerns – even if that means we cannot solve a problem. (Galloway 2007)

Opening up the discourse through critical design practice and a combination of highly situated ethics and aesthetics allows for greater critical manoeuvrability and means of progression into the future. The discussion in Chapter 3 showed how this affective function of critical design practice is being embraced in contexts of science and technology research where designers are collaborating with scientists, bioethicists, and even in environmental policy.

In a time when we are faced with rising complex societal problems, ethical sociotechnical questions, and material scarcity, there is need for a broad and more questioning form of design practice that serves to question and advance orthodox industrial design practice. We are now also at a point where we should question the impact of such practice. This is maybe where critical, speculative, and associative design falls short of its reach and impact to date. It is now established as a practice, and we should be confident in its disciplinary role, but we should now question and report on how critical design interfaces and impacts on the problem contexts it is used to engage with – how the debate, the engagement, the construction of publics, and the assembly of audience through the design device have meaningful effect. For example, how does it impact on the medical ethics it engages, the synthetic biologists who collaborate or reframe disciplinary attitudes towards production and consumption? How does it interface fully with the discourses it engages and how does it open itself effectively to challenge and critique in a context beyond critical design practice?

When we can evidence the impact and effect of critical design practice within the contexts that it is engaging, we can say that the purview and disciplinary remit of product and industrial design have been extended. We can say that critical and speculative design had an effect in how it has agitated and expanded the discipline.

But here we are met with a dilemma; when a critical design practice serves a utilitarian function and when it is incorporated into the disciplinary core and becomes part of the governing mentality, is it still critical? Perhaps not, but rest assured that other forms of critical practice will emerge that question the core and its governing mentalities just as associative, speculative, and critical design have done. The examples presented and the discussion in this book reflect on particular moments and approaches to critical practice. The taxonomy presents an interpretation and conceptual anchor to contextualize critical design practice, but critical practice is and always should be in flux and development for as long as the discipline and its governing mentalities are in flux and development.

NOTES

Chapter 1

1   Product and industrial design are used interchangeably throughout the book as terms used to define the product and industrial design discipline. Product design and industrial design are representative terms for the same subject. In the UK, product design is popularly used while internationally industrial design is used to describe the discipline, profession, and educational courses.

2   Boundary objects (artefacts, documents, vocabulary, film) help people from different communities build a shared understanding. Boundary objects will be interpreted differently by the different communities, and it is an acknowledgement and discussion of these differences that enables a shared understanding to be developed.

3   These comments were specifically made in the thread Design Practice 1: At the Design and Complexity Design Research Society Conference held at the University of Montréal, 2010. Over summer 2014, debate took place online as part of MoMA's *Design and Violence* curated discussion which challenged the insular discourse on critical and speculative design. Scholars including Cameron Tonkinwise (2014) have targeted their critique at the practices and its lack of engagement with discourse beyond art and design and how in within the practice designers are for the most part talking to themselves and peers. Tonkinwise's account appears at first critical of critical and speculative design practice. But this critique is delivered from a position that adds value to a critical practice. Tonkinwise through writing and public presentation calls for Speculative Critical Design to stand up to and address its critics. Moreover, he calls for Speculative Critical Design to engage discourses of critique and speculation outside of design epistemology. Looking beyond the disciplinary discourse, he calls into question the function of speculation and criticism and the impact that any design intervention might make and change that it might effect.

4   Examples of theoretical focus are illustrated by *CoDesign: The International Journal of CoCreation in Design and the Arts*, disseminating and problematizing participatory design. www.desis-network.org, an international project focusing on activity carried out in the field of design, led social innovation. Arguably, such dictated theoretical platforms focusing on critical design are yet to emerge.

Chapter 2

1   This describes a period of prosperity and mass consumption in the 1960s. In Italy, it was known as 'Bel Design' and in Germany 'Good Form'; it was a concept that ruled the mainstream design of large manufactures and the design output was rational and product orientated. The work was typified by the likes of Dieter Rams and Braun, Ettore Sottsass, and Olivetti.

Chapter 3

1   The Human Factors community aims to achieve 'fit' between human and object. See: Norman (1998). Technical function is perceived as the purposive and utilitarian value of an object it is expected to work in a particular way by the user through material and visual affordances.

2   In the 'Archaeology of Knowledge', Foucault attempted to find rules for how discourses are framed. For Foucault, discourse is not limited to disciplinary or linguistic discourse but entire ways of understanding things from various subjectivities. Discourse is perceived 'as a field of regularity for various positions of subjectivity' (2009, 59). Therefore, in practice, discourses allow for a certain way of seeing, understanding, and commenting, where one knows through discourse as they allow for the production of certain and individual truths.

3   For a discussion in this area, see Almquist and Lupton (2010).

4   For examples, see Gromala (1998); Hayles (2002); Gromala and Bolter (2005); Sterling (2005).

5   The contribution of STS to critical and speculative practice is evident in the scholars and designers subscribing to the theoretical tradition to ground their design research (Bleecker and Nova 2009; Kerridge 2009; Grand and Wiedmer, 2010; Wilkie 2010; Auger 2012).

6   The social and relational characteristics of design objects have been explored extensively in critical theories of technology and science studies e.g. Bijker (1995) explores the sociotechnical and political conditions that led to the development of the artefacts. A sociotechnical system is positioned as the interaction between society's complex infrastructures and human behaviours. In this sense, society itself and most of its substructures are complex sociotechnical systems.

Chapter 4

1   For examples of design practice in this area, see DiSalvo (2012).

2   See 'Practicing Science and Technology Performing the Social' (European Association for the Study of Science and Technology (EASST) conference, Trento, Italy, 3 September 2010).

3   See 'Ethnographic Fiction and Speculative Design' (5th International Conference on Communities & Technologies – C&T 2011, Brisbane, Australia, 29 June–2 July 2011).

4   See, for example, Mazé (2007), Moline (2006).

5   See, for example, Baudrillard (1996), Greenhalgh (1990), Kroes (2010), Krippendorf and Butter (1993), Papanek (1984), Schiffer (1992), Ligo (1984).

6   See, for example, Hällnas and Redström (2002), Dunne (1998), Balland Naylor (2006).

7   Wicked problems cannot be solved absolutely; the situation can only be made 'better' or 'worse' – the terms of which depend on who is evaluating the solution. For writing on wicked problems, see Rittel and Webber (1973). In a design context, see Buchanan (1992), Coyne (2005).

8   See Open IDEO: http://www.openideo.com/about-us

Chapter 5

1   An example often cited to illustrate the operation of juvenalian satire is Jonathan Swift's fable *A Modest Proposal*. Swift presents a solution to overpopulation and food shortage in eighteenth-century Ireland. He proposes to solve both these problems by reframing the problem as an opportunity. Through this reframing, the problem presents the means to solve itself. Swifts proposition suggests society should eat children and in so doing deal with food shortage and overpopulation. The fable draws attention to the issues at play through a logical solution infused with tones of obscenity and violence. The solution evokes outrage in the reader. Analogies can be drawn between the satiric strategies of violence and applied logic in Swift's satire and Dunne and Raby's invasive reengineering of human physiology to deal with overpopulation and food shortage and the ethical questions that the proposition evoke.

2   For further discussion on satire and satiric techniques, see Simpson (2003), Connery and Combe (1996).

BIBLIOGRAPHY

ATelier. 2011. *Design Things*. Cambridge, MA: MIT Press.

Adorno, Theodor. 1965. 'Functionalism Today. Originally Presented at the German Werkbund, Berlin, October 23, 1965'. *Reprinted Oppositions* 17: 30–41, Summer 1979.

Agre, Philip. 1997. *Computation and Human Experience*. Cambridge: Cambridge University Press.

Almquist, Julka, and Julia Lupton. 2010. 'Affording Meaning: Design-Oriented Research from the Humanities and Social Sciences'. *Design Issues* 26, no. 1: 3–14.

Ambaza, Emilio (ed.). 1972. *Italy: The New Domestic Landscape, Achievements and Problems of Italian Design*. New York: Museum of Modern Art.

Antonelli, Paola. 2010. 'Fresh as a Daisy: Alexandra Daisy Ginsberg'. *Nature Medicine* 16, no. 9: 942.

Archer, Bruce. 1995. 'The Nature of Research'. *Co-Design: Interdisciplinary Journal of Design* 2: 6–13.

Auger, James. 2010. 'Alternative Presents and Speculative Futures'. *Swiss Design Network Conference on Design Fictions Negotiating Futures*. Basel, Switzerland, 42–57.

Auger, James. 2012. *Why Robot? Speculative Design, the Domestication of Technology and the Considered Future PhD Diss*. London: Royal College of Art,

Auger, James, Laurel Swan, and Alex Taylor. 2010. 'Speculative Design by Practice – A Robot Case Study'. *European Association for the Study of Science and Technology (EASST) Conference*. Trento, Italy.

Bagha, Merhdad, Stephen Coley, and David White. 2000. *The Alchemy of Growth*. New York: Perseus Publishing.

Baird, George. 2004. 'Criticality and Its Discontents'. *Harvard Design Magazine* 21: 1–6.

Bakker, Gijs, and Renny Ramakers. 1998. *Droog Design: Spirit of the Nineties*. Rotterdam: 010 Publishers.

Ball, Ralph, and Maxine Naylor. 2006. *Form Follows Idea: An Introduction to Design Poetics*. London: Black Dog Publishing.

Baudrillard, Jean. 1981. *For a Critique of the Political Economy of the Sign*. Translated by Charles Levin. St Louis: Telos Press.

Baudrillard, Jean. 1996. *The System of Objects*. London: Verso.

Beaver, Jacob, Tobie Kerridge, and Sarah Pennington. 2009. *Material Beliefs*. London: Goldsmiths University of London Interaction Design Studio.

Betsky, Aron. 2003. 'The Strangeness of the Familiar in Design'. In *Strangely Familiar: Design and Everyday Life*, edited by Andrew Blauvelt, 14–37. Minneapolis, MN: Walker Art Center.

Bijker, Wiebe. 1995. *Of Bicycles, Bakelite, and Bulbs: Towards a Theory of Sociotechnical Change*. Cambridge, MA: MIT Press.

Bijker, Wiebe. 1992. 'The Social Construction of FLORESCENT Lighting or How an ARTEFACT Was Invented in Its Diffusion Stage'. In *Shaping Technology, Building Society*, edited by Wiebe Bijker and John Wiedmer, 75–102. Cambridge, MA: MIT Press.

Bijker, Wiebe, and John Law. 1994. *Shaping Technology/Building Society: Studies in Sociotechnical Change*. Cambridge, MA: MIT Press.

Billing, Jamie, and Tracy Cordingley. 2006. 'Some Kind of Analogtivity: Anti-Simulation Through Design'. *Personal and Ubiquitous Computing* (Springer-Verlag) 10, no. 2–3: 101–105.

Blauvelt, Andrew. 2008. *Towards Relational Design*. http://designobserver.com/feature/towards-relational-design/7557/ (accessed 29 July 2016).

Bleecker, Julian. 2010. 'Design Fiction: From Props to Prototypes'. *6th Swiss Design Network Conference 2010 Negotiating Futures Design Fiction*. Basel, Switzerland, 58–67.

Bleecker, Julian. 2004. *The Reality Effect of Technoscience PhD Diss*. Santa Cruz: University of California.

Bleecker, Julian, and Nicolas Nova. 2009. *A Synchronicity: Design Fictions for Asynchronous Urban Computing*. New York: The Architectural League of New York.

Boehner, Kirsten, Janet Vertesi, Phoebe Sengers, and Paul Dourish. 2007. 'How HCI Interprets the Probes'. *Proceedings of the SIGCHI Conference on Human Factors in Computing Systems*. San Jose, CA: ACM, 1077–1086.

Bonsiepe, Gui. 2007. 'The Uneasy Relationship between Design and Design Research'. In *Design Research Now*, edited by Ralf Michel, 25–39. Berlin: Birkhauser.

Brand, Stewart. 1988. *The Media Lab: Inventing the Future at MIT*. New York: Penguin.

Brandes, Uta, Sonja Stich, and Miriam Wender. 2009. *Design by Use: The Everyday Metamorphosis of Things*. Basel: Birkhauser.

Bredies, Katharina, Gesche Jooste, and Rosan Chow. 2009. 'Designers and Users: Comparing Constructivist Design Approaches'. *European Academy of Design: Design Connexity*. Aberdeen: Greys School of Art, 71–74.

Broms, Loove, Magnus Bång, and Sara Ilstedt Hjelm. 2008. 'Persuasive Engagement: Exploiting Lifestyle as a Driving Force to Promote Energy-Aware Use Patterns and Behaviours'. *Undisciplined! Design Research Society Conference 2008, 16–19 July 2008*. Sheffield: Sheffield Hallam University.

Buchanan, Richard. 1995. 'Branzi's Dilemma: Design in Contemporary Culture'. In *Design: Pleasure or Responsibility?* edited by Susann Vihma. Helsinki: University of Art and Design Helsinki.

Buchanan, Richard. 1989. 'Declaration by Design: Rhetoric, Argument and Demonstration in Design Practice'. In *Design Discourse*, edited by Victor Margolin, 91–109. Chicago, IL: University of Chicago Press.

Buchanan, Richard. 2001. 'Human Dignity and Human Rights: Thoughts on the Principles of Human Centred Design'. *Design Issues* 17, no. 3: 35–39.

Buchanan, Richard. 1992. 'Wicked Problems in Design Thinking'. *Design Issues* 8, no. 2: 5–215, 2009.

Bülmann, Vera. 2008. 'Pseudopodia. Prolegomena to a Discourse on Design'. In *Pre-Specifics: Some Comparatistic Investigations on Research in Design and Art*, edited by Vera Bülmann and Martin Wiedmer, 21–79. Zurich: JRP Ringer.

Burkhardt, François. 1988. 'Design and Avant-Postmodernism'. In *Design after Modernism*, edited by John Thackara, 145–151. London: Thames and Hudson.

Butler, Judith. 2002. 'What Is Critique? An Essay on Foucault's Virtue'. In *The Political: Readings in Continental Philosophy*, edited by David Ingram, 212–228. London, Basil: Blackwell.

Caccavale, Elio. 2010. *Future Families: A Practice Based Research Project to Explore Social, Cultural and Ethical Issues Surrounding Reproductive Technologies and New Family Forms*. http://www.rca.ac.uk/Default.aspx?ContentID=502274&GroupID=502 271&Contentwithinthissection&More=1 (accessed 15 September 2010).

Calhoun, Craig. 1995. *Critical Social Theory: Culture, History and the Challenge of Difference*. London: Blackwell.

Caputo, John D. 1987. *Radical Hermeneutics: Repetition, Deconstruction, and the Hermeneutic Project*. Bloomington: Indiana University Press.

Cogdell, Christina. 2009. 'Design and the Elastic Mind Museum of Modern Art (Spring 2008)'. *Design Issues* 25, no. 3: 92–101.

Coles, Alex. 2002. 'Art Décor: Art's Romance with Design'. *Art Monthly* 253.

Coles, Alex, ed. 2005. *Design Art*. London: Tate Publishing.

Coles, Alex, ed. 2007. *Design and Art*. Cambridge, MA: MIT Press.

Connery, B.A., and K. Combe (eds.). 1996. *Theorizing Satire: Essays in Criticism and Theory*. London: Palgrave Macmillan.

Coyne, Richard. 2005. 'Wicked Problems Revisited'. *Design Studies* 26, no. 1: 5–17.

Crampton Smith, Gillian. 1997. 'Computer Related Design at the Royal College of Art: 1997 Graduation Projects'. *Interactions* 4, no. 6: 27–33.

Crampton Smith, Gillian. 1994. 'The Art of Interaction'. In *Interacting with Virtual Environments*, edited by Lindsey MacDonald and John Vince. Hoboken, NJ: John Wiley & Sons.

Crampton Smith, Gillian, and Philip Tabor. 1996. 'The Role of the Artist Designer'. In *Bringing Design to Software*, edited by Terry Winograd, 35–57. Reading, MA: Addison Wesley.

Crisp, Denise Gonzales. 2009. 'Discourse This! Designers and Alternative Critical Writing'. *Design and Culture* (Berg) 1, no. 1: 105–120.

Critical Art Ensemble. http://www.critical-art.net (accessed 23 November 2010).

Cross, Nigel. 2001. 'Achieving Pleasure from Purpose: The Methods of Kenneth Grange Product Designer'. *The Design Journal* 4, no. 1: 48–58.

Cross, Nigel. 2002. 'Creative Cognition in Design: Processes of Exceptional Designers'. In *Creativity and Cognition*, edited by T. Hewett and T. Kavanah, 14–19. New York: ACM Press.

Cross, Nigel. 2006. *Designerly Ways of Knowing*. London: Springer Verlag Ltd.

Cross, Nigel. 2007. 'From a Design Science to a Design Discipline: Understanding Designerly Ways of Knowing'. In *Design Research Now. Essays and Selected Projects*, edited by Ralf Michel, 41–54. Basel, Boston, Berlin: Birkhäuser Verlag AG.

Design Act. 2009. (accessed 25 August 2011).

Design and the Elastic Mind. *Design and the Elastic Mind MoMA*. http://www.moma.org/interactives/exhibitions/2008/elasticmind/ (accessed 26 September 2011).

Design for Thought: Contemporary Product Design from Britain. 2005. http://www.imj.org.il/eng/exhibitions/2005/design_for_thought/pop/popnoir.html (accessed 14 August 2010).

Design Interactions RCA. 2011. http://www.di.research.rca.ac.uk/content/about (accessed 29 July 2016).

Dialogues in Design: *Design as a Medium*. 2010, 02–03. http://dialoguesindesign.wordpress.com/2010/02/16/next-session-design-as-a-medium-tuesday-2nd-march/ (accessed 16 September 2011).

DiSalvo, Carl. 2012. *Adversarial Design*. Cambridge, MA: MIT Press.

DiSalvo, Carl. 2009. 'Design and the Construction of Publics'. *Design Studies* (Massachusetts Institute of Technology) 25, no. 1: 48–63.

Dormer, Peter. 1990. *The Meanings of Modern Design*. London: Thames & Hudson.

Dunne, Anthony. 1997. *Hertzian Tales: An Investigation into the Critical Potential of Electronic Product as a Post-Optimal Object PhD Diss*. London: Royal College of Art.

Dunne, Anthony. 1998. *Hertzian Tales: Electronic Products, Aesthetic Experience and Critical Design*. London: Royal College of Art Computer Related Design Research Publications.

Dunne, Anthony. 2010. 'Revitalizing Design: Revital Cohen'. *Nature Medicine* 16, no. 9: 944.

Dunne, Anthony, and Fiona Raby. 2014. *Speculative Everything: Design, Fiction, and Social Dreaming*. Cambridge: MIT Press.

Dunne, Anthony, and Fiona Raby. 2008. 'A/B'. http://www.dunneandraby.co.uk/content/projects/476/0 (accessed 3 August 2015).

Dunne, Anthony, and Fiona Raby. 2003. *Consuming Monsters: Big, Perfect, Infectious*. London: Unpublished.

Dunne, Anthony, and Fiona Raby. 2002. 'The Placebo Project'. *DIS '02: Proceedings of the 4th Conference on Designing Interactive Systems: Processes, Practices, Methods, and Techniques*. ACM Press, 11–14.

Dunne, Anthony, and Fiona Raby. 2001. *Design Noir: The Secret Life of Electronic Objects*. London: August/Birkhauser.

Dunne, Anthony, Revital Cohen, and Alice Wang. 2008. *Index Design Interactions*. London: Royal College of Art.

Ericson, Magnus, and Ramia Mazé, 2011. *DESIGN ACT Socially and Politically Engaged Design Today – Critical Roles and Emerging Tactics*. Stockholm: Sternberg Press.

ESPRC, RCA, NESTA. *Impact Exhibition*. 2010. http://www.epsrc.ac.uk/newsevents/events/impactexhibition/Pages/default.aspx (accessed 20 November 2010).

Fallman, Daniel. 2003. 'Design-Oriented Human-Computer Interaction'. *CHI Letters* 5, no. 1: 225–232.

Fallman, Daniel. 2008. 'The Interaction Design Research Triangle of Design Practice, Design Studies, and Design Exploration'. *Design Studies* (Massachusetts Institute of Technology) 24, no. 3: 4–18.

Feenberg, Andrew. 1999. *Questioning Technology*. London: Routledge.

Feenberg, Andrew. 2002. *Transforming Technology: A Critical Theory Revisited*. New York: Oxford University Press.

Findeli, A. 1998. 'A Quest for Credibility: Doctoral Education in Design at the University of Montreal'. *Doctoral Education in Design*. Ohio, 8–11.

Findeli, A., and R Bousbaci. 2005. 'The Eclipse of the Object in Design Project Theories'. *The Design Journal* 8, no. 3: 35–49.

Findelli, A. 2008. 'Research Through Design and Transdisciplinarity: A Tentative Contribution to the Methodology of Design Research'. *Proceedings of Swiss Design Network Symposium*. Berne Switzerland.

Fischer, Michael. 2006. Science Technology and Society. In *Theory Culture and Society: Problematizing Global Knowledge*, Vol. 23, edited by Mike Featherstone, Venn Couze, Ryan Bishop and John Phillips, 172–174. London: Sage.

Fisher, Tom, and Janet Shipton. 2010. *Designing for Re-use*. London: Earthscan.

Floyd, Christine. 2005. 'Being Critical in, on or Around Computing'. *Proceedings of the 4th Decennial Conference on Critical Computing: Between Sense and Sensibility, Aarhus, Denmark, August 20–24, 2005*. New York: ACM, 207–211.

Flusser, Vilem. 1999. 'About the Word Design'. In *The Shape of Things: A Philosophy of Design*. London: Reaktion Books.

Forlizzi, J., E. Stolterman, and J. Zimmerman. 2009. 'From Design Research to Theory: Evidence of a Maturing Field'. *Proceedings of the International Association of Societies of Design Research*. IASDR.

Foster, Hal. 2002. *Design and Crime: and other Diatribes*. London: Verso.

Foucault, Michel. 2009. *The Archaeology of Knowledge*. London: Routledge.

Foucoult, Michel. 2002. 'What Is Critique?' In *The Political*, edited by David Ingram, 191–211. Oxford: Blackwell.

Franke, Björn. 2009. 'Design as a Medium for Inquiry'. *Fifth Swiss Design Network Symposium*, *Multiple Ways to Design Research – Research Cases That Reshape the Design Discipline*. Swiss Design Network, 225–232.

Frayling, Christopher. 1993. 'Research in Art and Design'. *Royal College of Art Research Papers* (Royal College of Art) 1, no. 1: 1–5.

Friedman, Ken. 2003. 'Theory Construction in Design Research: Criteria: Approaches, and Methods'. *Design Studies* 24: 507–522.

Fulton Suri, J. 2007. 'Involving People in the Process'. *Include 2007 Conference*. London: RCA.

Galloway, Anne. 2007. 'Design Research as Critical Practice'. *Presented at the Carleton University Industrial Design 29th Annual Seminar*. Ottawa.

Gamman, Lorraine, and Adam Thorpe, 2011. 'Design with Society: Why Socially Responsive Design Is Good Enough'. *CoDesign: International Journal of CoCreation in Design and the Arts* 7 no. 3–4: 217–230.

Gardien, Paul. 2006. 'Breathing Life into Delicate Ideas, Position Paper, Philips Design'. *Philips Design*. http://www.design.philips.com/shared/assets/design_assets/downloads/news/Breathing_life_into_delicate_ideas.pdf (accessed 15 December 2010).

Gaver, William, Michael, Mike, Kerridge, Tobie, Wilkie, Alex, Boucher, Andy, Ovalle, Liliana, and Plummer-Fernandez, Matthew. 2015. 'Energy Babble: Mixing Environmentally-Oriented Internet Content to Engage Community Groups'. *Proceedings of the SIGCHI Conference on Human Factors in Computing Systems*. Seoul, Republic of Korea, April 18–23.

Gaver, W., et al. 2004. 'The Drift Table: Designing for Ludic Engagement'. *CHI '04*.

Gaver, William, and Anthony Dunne. 1997. 'The Pillow: Artist Designers in the Digital Age'. *CHI '97 Extended Abstracts on Human Factors in Computing Systems: Looking to the Future*. ACM.

Gaver, William, and Heather Martin. 2000. 'Alternatives: Exploring Information Appliances Through Conceptual Design Proposals'. *Human Factors in Computing Systems (CHI)*. New York: ACM Press, 209–216.

Gaver, William, Jake Beaver, and Steve Benford. 2003. 'Ambiguity as a Resource for Design'. *Conference on Human Factors in Computing Systems (CHI)*. New York: ACM Press, 233–240.

Geertz, C.N. 1973. *The Interpretation of Cultures*. New York: Basic Books.

Ginsberg, Alexander Daisy, J. Calvert, P. Schyfter, A Elfick, and A.D. Endy. 2014. *Synthetic Aesthetics: Investigating Synthetic Biology's Designs on Nature*. Cambridge: MIT Press.

Ginsberg, Alexander Daisy. 2010. 'The Synthetic Kingdom'. *Second Nature: International Journal of Creative Media* 2, no. 1: 266–284.

Glaser, B., and A. Strauss. 1967. *The Discovery of Grounded Theory: Strategies for Qualitative Research*.

Grand, Simon. 2010. 'Research as Design: Future Perspectives'. In *The Future of Design Research*, edited by Wolfgang Jonas, Simon Grand, and Ralf Michel. Basel, Boston, Berlin: Birkhäuser Verlag AG.

Grand, Simon, and Martin Wiedmer. 2010. 'Design Fiction: A Method Toolbox for Design Research in a Complex World'. *Proceedings of Design and Complexity Design Research Society*. Montréal: Ecol de design industrial. Univeritie de.

Green, Josephine. 2007. 'Democratizing the Future: Towards a New Era of Creativity and Growth'. design.philips.com. http://www.design.philips.com/shared/assets/ Downloadablefile/democratizing-the-future-14324.pdf (accessed 16 February 2011).

Greenhalgh, Paul. 1990. *Modernism in Design*. London: Reaktion Books.

Gromala, D, and Jay David Bolter. 2005. *Windows and Mirrors: Interaction Design, Digital Art, and the Myth of Transparency*. Cambridge: MA.

Gromala, D. 1998. 'Abject Subjectivities'. in American Center for Design. Remaking History: The Convergence of Graphic Design, History, Theory, and Criticism for Creative Practice. Chicago, IL: American Center for Design, February 28, March 1 & 2, 1997, 6–11.

Hällnas, Lars, and Johan Redström. 2002a. 'From Use to Presence: On Expressions and Aesthetics of Everyday Computational Things'. *ACM Transactions on Computational Things* 9, no. 2: 106–124.

Hällnas, Lars, and Johan Redström. 2002b. 'Abstract Information Appliances: Methodological Exercises in Conceptual Design of Computational Things'. *Proceedings of the Conference on Designing Interactive Systems: Processes, Practices, Methods and Techniques*. New York: ACM Press, 105–116.

Hällnas, Lars, and Johan Redström. 2001. 'Slow Technology: Designing for Reflection'. *Journal of Personal and Ubiquitous Computing* 5, no. 3: 201–212.

Hayles, K. 2002. *Writing Machines*. Cambridge, MA: MIT Press, Mediawork Pamphlet Series.

Hunt, Jamer. 2003. 'Just Re-Do It: Tactical Formlessness and Everyday Consumption'. In *Strangely Familiar: Design and Everyday Life*, edited by Andrew Blauvelt, 56–71. Minneapolis: Walker Art Centre.

Hunt, Jamer. 2011. 'Prototyping the Social: Temporality and Speculative Futures at the Intersection of Design and Culture'. In *Design Anthropology: Object Culture in the 21st Century*, edited by Alison J. Clarke, 33–44. New York: Springer Wien.

IDEO. *Open IDEO*. http://www.openideo.com/about-us (accessed 20 September 2011).

Jenks, Charles, and Nathan Silver. 1972. *Adhocism: The Case for Improvisation*. New York: Doubleday.

Jeremijenko, Natalie, and Eugene Thacker. 2004. *Creative Biotechnology*. Newcastle upon Tyne: Locus+ Publishing Ltd.

Jonas, Wolfgang. 2007. 'Design Research and Its Meaning to the Methodological Development of the Discipline'. In *Design Research Now*, edited by Ralf Michel, 187–205. Berlin: Birkhauser Verlag.

Julier, Guy. 2006. 'From Visual Culture to Design Culture'. *Design Issues* (MIT Press) 22, no. 1: 64–76.

Julier, Guy. 2000. *The Culture of Design*. London: Sage.

Kerridge, Tobie. 2015. *Designing Debate: The Entanglement of Speculative Design and Upstream Engagement Doctoral Thesis*. London: Goldsmiths, University of London.

Kerridge, Tobie. 2009. 'Does Speculative Design Contribute to the Engagement of Science and Technology'. *Multiple Pathways: Swiss Design Network Symposium*. Lugano, Switzerland.

Kirby, David. 2010. 'The Future Is Now: Diegetic Prototypes and the Role of Popular Films in Generating Real-World Technological Development'. *Social Studies of Science* 40, no. 1: 41–70.

Knorr Cetina, K. 1999. *Epistemic Cultures: How the Sciences Make Knowledge*. Cambridge, MA: MIT Press.

Koskinen, I., J. Zimmerman, T. Binder, and S. Wensveen. 2011. *Design Research Through Practice. From the Lab, Field, and Showroom*. London: Morgan Kaufman.

Krippendorff, Klaus. 2006. *The Semantic Turn: A New Foundation for Design*. London: Taylor & Francis.

Krippendorff, Klaus, and Reihhart Butter. 1993. 'Where Meanings Escape Functions'. *Design Management Institute Journal* 4, no. 2: 30–37.

Krippendorff, Klause. 2006. *Content Analysis: An Introduction to Its Methodology*. London: Sage.

Krippendorff, Klause. 2007. 'Design Research: An Oxymoron?' In *Design Research Now: Essays and Selected Projects*, edited by Ralf Michel, 67–80. Basel, Boston, Berlin: Birkhäuser Verlag AG.

Kroes, Peter. 2010. 'Theories of Technical Functions: Function Ascriptions vs. Function Assignments Part 2'. *Design Issues* 24, no. 4: 85–93.

Lang, Peter, and William Menking. 2003. *Superstudio: Life Without Objects*. Milan: Skira Editore.

Latour, Bruno. 2009. 'A Cautious Prometheus? A Few Steps towards a Philosophy of Design (with Special Attention to Peter Sloterdijk)'. Edited by J. Glynne, F. Hackney, and V. Minton. *Networks of Design: Proceedings of the 2008 Annual Conference of the Design History Society (UK)*. Online: Universal Publishers, 2–10.

Latour, Bruno. 1993. *We Have Never Been Modern*. Cambridge, MA: Harvard University Press.

Lees-Maffei, Grace, and Kjetil Fallan. 2014. 'Introduction: The History of Italian Design'. In *Made in Italy: Rethinking a Century of Italian Design*, edited by Grace Lees-Maffei and Kjetil Fallan, 22–79. London: Bloomsbury Academic.

Lemoine, Philippe. 1988. 'The Demise of Classic Rationality'. In *Design after Modernism*, edited by John Thackara, 187–196. London: Thames and Hudson.

Ligo, Larry L. 1984. *The Concept of Function in Twentieth-Century Architectural Criticism*. Ann Arbor, MI: UMI Research Press.

Löwgren, Jonas, and Erik Stolterman. 2007. *Thoughtful Interaction Design: A Design Perspective on Information Technology*. Cambridge, MA: MIT Press.

Maldonado, Tomás. 1972. *Design, Nature, and Revolution; Toward a Critical Ecology*. New York: Harper & Row.

Malpass, Matt. 2009. 'Contextualising Critical Design: A Classification of Critical Practice in Design'. *Proceedings of Design Connexity Eighth European Academy of Design Conference*. Aberdeen: Gray's School of Art and Design, The Robert Gordon University, 289–293.

Malpass, Matt. 2010. 'Perspectives on Critical Design: A Conversation with Ralph Ball and Maxine Naylor'. *Proceedings of Design and Complexity Design Research Society*. Montréal: Ecol de design industrial. Univeritie de Montréal.

Malpass, Matt. 2011. 'Critical Design and a History of Marginalised Practice'. *Design History Society Conference on Design Activism*. Barcelona.

Malpass, Matt. 2012. *Contextualising Critical Design: Towards a Taxonomy of Critical Practice in Product Design PhD Diss*. School of Architecture Design and Built Environment: Nottingham, Trent University.

Malpass, Matt. 2013. 'Between Wit and Reason: Defining Associative, Speculative and Critical Design in Practice'. *Design and Culture* 5, no. 4.

Malpass, Matt. 2015. 'Criticism and Function in Critical Design Practice'. *Design Issues* 31, no. 4: 59–73.

Mazé, Ramia. 2007. *Occupying Time: Design, Technology, and the Form of Interaction*. Stockholm: Axl Books.

Mazé, Ramia, and Johan Redström. 2007. 'Difficult Forms: Critical Practices in Design and Research'. *Proceedings of the Conference of the International Association of Societies of Design Research*. Hong Kong: IASDR.

Mermoz, Gérard. 2006. 'The Designer as Author: Reading the City of Signs – Istanbul'. *Design Issues* 22, no. 2: 77–87.

Michael, M. 2012. 'What Are We Busy Doing?': Engaging the Idiot'. *Science, Technology, & Human Values* 37, no. 5: 528–554.

Miller, Daniel. 2001. 'Disciplinary Approaches to Consumption'. In *Consumption and Critical Concepts in the Social Sciences*, edited by Daniel Miller, 1–4. London: Routledge.

Miller, Daniel. 1987. *Material Culture and Mass Consumption*. New York: Blackwell.

Moline, Katherine. 2006. 'Authorship, Entrepreneurialism and Experimental Design'. *Visual: Design:Scholarship. The Research Journal of the Australian Graphic Design Association* 2, no. 2: 57–66.

Moline, Katherine. 2008. 'Counter-Forces in Experimental Design: H Edge and the Technological Dreams Series #1 (Robots)'. *Studies in Material Thinking* 1, no. 2: www.materialthinking.org/volume-1-issue2.php

Muller, Michael, Daniel Wildman, and Ellen White. 1993. 'Taxonomy of PD Practices: A Brief Practitioners Guide'. *Communications of the ACM* 36, no. 4: 25–28.

Myerson, J., and Y Lee. 2011. 'Designing for the People, with the People, and by the People'. *Design History Society Conference on Design Activism*. Barcelona.

Nelson, Harold, and Erik Stolterman. 2012. *The Design Way: Intentional Change in an Unpredictable World*. Cambridge, MA: MIT Press.

Niedderer, Kristina. 2006. 'Designing Mindful Interaction: The Category of Performative Object'. *Design Issues* (The MIT Press) 23, no. 1: 3–17.

Niedderer, Kristina. 2004. *Designing the Performative Object: A Study in Designing Mindful Interaction Through Artefacts PhD Diss*. Falmouth: Faculty of Culture & Media Falmouth College of Arts.

Nieusma, Dean. 2004. 'Alternative Design Scholarship: Working toward Appropriate Design'. *Design Issues* 20, no. 3: 13–24.

Norman, Donald. 1998. *The Design of Everyday Things*. 3. London: MIT Press.

Palmer, Jerry, and Mo Dodson, 1996. *Design and Aesthetics*. London: Routledge.

Papanek, Victor. 1984. *Design for the Real World*. 2. London: Thames and Hudson.

Pierce, J., and E. Paulos. 2014. 'Counterfunctional Things: Exploring Possibilities in Designing Digital Limitations'. *DIS '14*.

Potter, J., and M Wetherall. 1994. 'Analysing Discourse'. In *Analysing Qualitative Data*, edited by A. Bryman and R. Burgess, 47–68. London: Routledge.

Potter, Norman. 2002. *What Is a Designer: Things, Places and Messages*. London: Hyphen Press.

Poynor, R. 2005. *Art's Little Brother Icon 023* (accessed 22 October 2009).

Poynor, Rick. 2008. 'All That Is Graphic Melts into Air … Design Art and the Art of Design'. *Proceedings of the Symposium AC|DC Contemporary Art Contemporary Design, 26–27 October 2007*. Geneva: Geneva University of Art and Design, 34–45.

Poynor, Rick. 1999. 'Made in Britain: The Ambiguous Image'. In *Lost & Found: Critical Voices in New British Design*, edited by Nick Barley. The British Council.

Prina, Daniela. 2008. 'Design as Conceptual Research and Political Instrument: Role and Legacy of the Italian Radical Movement'. *Networks of Design: Proceedings of the 2008 Annual International Conference of the Design History Society*. Falmouth: University College Falmouth, 100–106.

Pullin, Graham. 2010. 'Curating and Creating Design Collections from Social Mobiles to the Museum of Lost Interactions and Six Speaking Chairs'. *Design and Culture* 2, no. 3: 309–328.

Pullin, Graham. 2007. 'Social Mobiles and Speaking Chairs'. *EAD 07 Dancing with Disorder: Design Discourse Disaster*, 726–731.

Raby, Fiona. 2008. 'Critical Design'. In *Design Dictionary: Perspective on Design Terminology*, edited by Michael Erlhof and Tim Marshall, 94–96. Boston: Birkhauser.

Ramakers. 2002. *Less + More: Droog Design in Context*. Rotterdam: 010 Publishers.

Ratto, Matt. 2011. 'Critical Making: Conceptual and Material Studies in Technology and Social Life'. *The Information Society* 27, no. 4: 252–260.

Ratto, Matt, and Megan Boler, 2014. *DIY Citizenship: Critical Making and Social Media*. Cambridge, MA: MIT Press.

Redström, Johan. 2008. 'Aesthetic Concerns in Pervasive Information Systems'. In *Pervasive Information Systems: Advances in Management Information Systems*, edited by Panos E. Kourouthanassis and George M. Giaglis, 197–209. New York: M.E. Sharpe.

Redström, Johan. 2006. 'Towards User Design? On the Shift from Object to User as the Subject of Design'. *Design Studies* 27: 123–39.

REF. 2014. 'Critical Design at the Royal College of Art and Its Impact on Design and the Public Understanding of Science'. *REF 2014 Impact Case Studies*. Royal College of Art. 2014. http://impact.ref.ac.uk/CaseStudies/CaseStudy.aspx?Id=44132 (accessed 20 June 2015).

Rendell, Jane, Jonathan Hill, Murray Fraser, and Mark Dorrian, 2007. *Critical Architecture*. New York: Routledge.

Rittel, H., and M. Webber. 1973. 'Dilemmas in a General Theory of Planning'. *Policy Sciences* 4: 155–169.

Robach, Cilla. 2005. 'Critical Design: Forgotten History or Paradigm Shift'. In *Shift: Design as Usual-Or a New Rising?*, edited by Lars Dencik, 30–41. Stockholm: Arvinius.

Rossi, Catharine. 2013. 'Bricolage, Hybridity, Circularity: Crafting Production Strategies in Critical and Conceptual Design'. *Design and Culture* 5, no. 1: 69–87.

Sanders, E., and P. Stappers. 2008. 'Co-Creation and the New Landscapes of Design'. *CoDesign. Co-Creation and the New Landscapes of Design* 4, no. 1: 5–18.

Sanders, Elizabeth. 2006. 'Design Research Society'. *Design Research in 2006. Design Research Quarterly* 1, no. 1: 1–8.

Scanlan, Joe. 2001. 'Please, Eat the Daisies' *Art Issues* (January/February 2001): 26.

Schön, Donald. 1983. *The Reflective Practitioner: How Professionals Think in Action*. New York: Basic Books.

Schiffer, Michael. 1992. *The Material Life of Human Beings: Artefacts Behaviour and Communication*. London: Routledge.

Schiffer, Michael B. 1992. *Technological Perspectives on Behavioural Change*. Tuscan, AZ: University of Arizona Press.

Scholz, Gudrun. 1989. 'Where Is the Designer on Identity and Plurality'. In *Die Macht der Gegenstande. Designtheorie 3 Essays*. Vol. 89, 1–108, Berlin: Hochschule der Künste Berlin.

Seago, Alex, and Anthony Dunne. 1999. 'New Methods in Art and Design Research: The Object as Discourse'. *Design Issues* 15, no. 2: 11–17.

Sengers, Phoebe. 2005. 'Reflective Design'. *CC'05: Proceedings of the 4th Decennial Conference on Critical Computing*. New York: ACM Press, 49–58.

Sengers, Phoebe, John McCarthy, and Paul Dourish. 2006. 'Reflective HCI: Articulating an Agenda for Critical Practice'. *The Conference on Human Factors in Computing Systems (CHI)*. New York: ACM Press, 1683–1686.

Shove, Elizabeth, Matthew Watson, and Jack Ingram. 2007. *The Design of Everyday Life: Cultures of Consumption*. London: Berg.

Schuler, Douglas, and Aki Namioka. 1993. *Participatory Design: Principles and Practices*. Hillsdale, NJ: Lawrence Erlbaum.

Simpson, P. 2003. *On the Discourse of Satire: Towards a Stylistic Model of Satirical Humor Linguistic Approaches to Literature*. London: John Benjamin Publishers Company.

Snodgrass, Adrian, and Richard Coyne. 1997. 'Is Designing Hermeneutical?' *Architectural Theory Review Journal of the Department of Architecture* (The University of Sydney) 1, no. 1: 11–17.

Sparke, Penny. 2014. 'Ettore Sottsass and Critical Design in Italy, 1965–1985'. In *Made in Italy: Rethinking a Century of Italian Design*, edited by Grace Lees-Maffei and Kjetil Fallan, 112–135. London: Bloomsbury Academic.

Sterling, Bruce. 2005. *Shaping Things*. Cambridge: MIT Press Mediawork Pamphlet Series.

Studiolab. 2011. 'StudioLab – A New European Platform for Creative Interactions between Art and Science'. *European Commission CORDIS*. http://cordis. europa.eu/search/index.cfm?fuseaction=proj.document&PJ_LANG=EN&PJ_ RCN=12114084&pid=3 (accessed 9 August 2011).

Sullivan, Louis H. 1896. 'The Tall Office Building Artistically Considered'. *Lippincott's Monthly Magazine*, LVII.

Thackara, John. 1988. *Design after Modernism: Beyond the Object*. New York: Thames and Hudson.

Thackara, John. 2005. *In the Bubble: Designing in a Complex World*. Cambridge, MA: MIT Press.

Tharp, Bruce, and Stephanie Tharp. 2008. 'Discursive Design: Beyond Purely Commercial Notions of Industrial/Product Design'. *IDSA National Education Symposium Proceedings*. Phoenix Arizona.

Tharp, Bruce, and Stephanie Tharp. 2008. The 4 Fields of Industrial Design: (No, not furniture, trans, consumer electronics, & toys) http://www.core77.com/posts/12232/ the-4-fields-of-industrial-design-no-not-furniture-trans-consumer-electronics-toys-by- bruce-m-tharp-and-stephanie-m-tharp-12232 (accessed 29 July 2016).

The Interactive Institute. 2004–05. http://www.tii.se/static/index.htm (accessed 20 November 2010).

The Interactive Institute. 2007. *Switch*. http://www.tii.se/switch (accessed 20 November 2010).

Tonkinwise, Cameron, Terry Irwin, Gideon Kossoff, and Peter Scupelli. 2015. 'Transition Design 2015: A New Area of Design Research, Practice and Study That Proposes Design-Led Societal Transition toward More Sustainable Futures'. *School of Design Carnegie Mellon University*. School of Design Carnegie Mellon University. http:// design.cmu.edu/sites/default/files/Transition_Design_Monograph_final.pdf (accessed 8 October 2015).

Tufte, Edward. 2001. *The Visual Display of Quantitative Information*. 2. Cheshire, CT: Graphics Press.

van de Poel, Ibo, and Peter Kroes. 2006. 'Technology and Normativity'. *Techné: Research in Philosophy and Technology* 10, no. 1: 1–6.

Von Hipplel, Eric. 2005. *Democratizing Innovation*. Cambridge: MIT Press.

Walker, Stewart. 2006. *Sustainable by Design: Explorations in Theory and Practice*. London: Earthscan.

Walker, Stuart. 2010. 'Wrapped Attention: Designing Products for Evolving Permanence and Enduring Meaning'. *Design Issues* 26, no. 4: 94–108.

Wang, Alice. 2009. 'Asimov's First Law/Alarm Clocks'. *Proceedings of the Third International Conference on Tangible and Embedded Interaction (TEI'09), Cambridge, UK*. ACM, 31–34.

Ward, Matt, and Alex Wilki. 2009. 'Made in Critical Land: Designing Matters of Concern'. In *Networks of Design: Proceedings of the 2008 Annual Conference of the Design History Society (UK)*, edited by Jonathan Glynne, Fiona Hackney and Viv Minton, 118–124. Universal Publishers.

Whiteley, Nigel. 1993. *Design for Society*. London: Reaktion Books.

Wiel, Daniel. 1994. *Design Renaissance: Selected Papers from the International Design Congress 1993 Glasgow*. Edited by Jeremy Myerson. London: Open Eye Publishing.

Wilkie, A. 2010. *User Assemblages in Design: An Ethnographic Study*. PhD Diss. London: Goldsmiths University of London.

Wodiczko, Krzysztof. 1999. *Critical Vehicles: Writings, Projects, Interviews*. Cambridge, MA: MIT Press.

Zimmerman, J., E. Stolterman, and J. Forlizzi. 2010. 'An Analysis and Critique of Research through Design: Toward a Formalization of a Research Approach'. *Proceedings of the 8th ACM Conference on Designing Interactive Systems (DIS'10)*.

INDEX